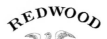

MISTRESS OF VERSAILLES

Madame Du Barry by Drouais

Mistress of Versailles

THE LIFE OF
MADAME DU BARRY

Agnes de Stoeckl

JOHN MURRAY

Foreword

In this book I shall not delve into the heavy, complicated political aspect of Louis XV's reign of which every detail has been expounded. As this is surely my last book – I am well over ninety-one years old – I intend to dedicate it to myself and forget that other people may criticize! I shall not follow all the authors who copy one another but give free rein to my knowledge of Court life, of Versailles, of Courtesans, of my youth, of the *légèreté* of the French nation. I shall keep it historically true, but will give the human side of that wonderful France which at times has been led by the devil and his horrors, but which in repentance created the marvellous church Le Sacré Coeur at Montmartre which dominates and blesses Paris.

Many of my readers may deplore the omission of several persons who were connected with my heroine, but my ambition is that she should stand alone, a unique being, unfettered by a host of appendages. She was beautiful, kind, thoughtless of the future. She never lost that primitive *largesse* which is the privilege of those whose every wish has ever been granted. In the eyes of the world she may have sinned, but few, if any, have ever achieved her great act of charity. 'She gave her life for a friend.'

Contents

Illustrations

Acknowledgements

I should like to express my deepest gratitude to Mrs. Pacey Blauwers for her constant, kind and charming help during the two years which this book has taken to write. Her patience has been heroic and her friendship the source of great encouragement when my great age loomed before me.

✤   ✤   ✤

I would like to thank Monsieur Van der Kemp, Conservateur en Chef du Musée de Versailles, for his kindness in advising me in the work of research.

I also thank the late Mr. Wilfred Edwards for his graciousness in revising this book, and Mr. John Gibbins for his invaluable help.

I cannot think of anybody else to thank except myself!

Prelude

Versailles – April 1764

The rain had turned into a cataract, it dimmed the view of the palatial glory; from a side entrance a small convoy emerged; it accompanied the body of the most renowned woman of the era – the Marquise de Pompadour, despotic mistress of the King for the past twenty years. It was conveying her to the vaults of the convent of the Capucines, Place Vendôme, where slowly she would crumble into dust. No fuss, no crowd, only one or two officials who stood in the wet to speed the departure of the unassuming procession.

From a window, partly hidden by a curtain, a man watched impatiently, no tears, no sighs, no prayer, just a murmur – 'The poor Marquise has bad weather for her last journey,' thus was Louis XV's farewell.

1768

Four years had elapsed since the day the rain in its deluge seemed to weep for the passing of a great woman, four years of apparent morality. His Majesty had as yet no official mistress; although this scandalous distinction had been besieged shamelessly and fiercely, the fortress had remained impenetrable.

The Queen Marie Leczinska had hoped and prayed that her husband might have forsaken for ever the outrageous life which he had led for so many years. Yet although he was no longer under the spell of an established mistress, he did not return to her. She often wondered, had he forgotten the many years of conjugal happiness, and close relationship? Six daughters and two sons had been born during these happy years. The Court had often marvelled at such a miracle of faithfulness. The true reason for Louis XV's attachment to his wife had been his natural indolence, this apathy had saved the royal marriage.

Louis XV was almost too beautiful and the added glory of the crown of France made him stand out like a divinity, which captivated the world. In his *Mémoires secrètes pour servir a l'Histoire de Perse*, Cha-Sephi describes Louis XV thus – 'At the age of sixteen to seventeen Louis XV was like Adonis reborn, of noble bearing, of a splendid height, his limbs ideally proportioned, from his almond-shaped eyes a gentle look would captivate all those approaching him, his delicate health added to all this, languid grace. His education had been neglected for fear of tiring him, but encircled by the culture of France he imbibed in time a certain knowledge of intellectual matters which atoned for much which he had never been taught.'

Negotiations had taken place for some time with the Court of

Spain concerning a child Infanta as future spouse for Louis XV. The one condition was that she should be educated in France so as to fit her for her coming role. She arrived accompanied by her Court and was sumptuously lodged at the Tuileries. Louis and she never met, all was still so remote since there was so much time to spare. She was eight years old when unexpectedly the young King fell ill with a feverish attack. The whole of France shuddered with terror, supposing the boy died without leaving an heir? What would become of the Kingdom with all its different factions? A nubile wife must be found at once. The Duc de Bourbon, the Prime Minister, commanded that the Infanta should be returned to Spain without delay – which offended that country. The case was too urgent to stop at such paltry considerations. The Duc ordered a list to be drawn up of all available princesses on the market, one hundred names were submitted. Forty-four were deleted for various reasons – some not yet nubile, some whose birth did not equal the King's rank, others of different faiths from the King. So from reduction to reduction only four possibilities remained – two daughters of George I, the King of England, who would on no account change their religion – the daughter of Catherine I of Russia of whom the Bourbons could not even contemplate the idea since the Empress had been a tavern maid in her youth – and lastly Marie Leczinska, who was twenty-two at the time and whose father, King Stanislas, had sat for a while on the Polish throne. This gave her a Royal connection, and she became the chosen one. The Painter Gobert, who was sent to paint her portrait, describes her thus: 'The Princess is short of stature, with a good figure and she walks well, her hair is chestnut, her eyebrows well designed and rainbow shaped, her eyes are deeply set, not very large, but fine and vivacious, her cheeks are full and delicately coloured, her nose is rather long but well shaped, her mouth is neither large nor small, with deep red lips, her neck is well proportioned, and her shoulders well placed, and her bosom is high and white. She is refined and gracious, and has a quick wit. She is very cultured, not proud, exceedingly charitable and generous in the extreme. In fact the Princess is a paragon of virtue. Her father and his little Court live scantily with bare comforts, the whole atmosphere expresses necessity of every kind, yet the King never complains. As far as I could judge, the situation is thus, King Stanislas and Princess Marie are pleased at the idea of her becoming Queen of France, but they retained their dignity.' This satisfied the young King.

On the 27th May 1725 Louis XV announced at his *lever* his betrothal to the Princess Marie Leczinska, he was fifteen years old! When the surprise of this extraordinary news died down, jealousies were nurtured in every breast, and attempts to thwart this inconceivable alliance sprang from every side. Nevertheless the marriage by proxy took place in Strasbourg on the 15th of August.

The King's tutors were now confronted with the delicate mission of instructing him in the consummation of the marital act. A conference took place, no time was to be lost. They agreed the best way to enlighten the young King would be to hang a series of pictures in his study to instruct him on the subject. The King was quick to understand!

Louis XV travelled to Fontainebleau to meet his bride. As he approached, the Queen left her carriage and knelt down to kiss his hand, but he raised her and kissed her on both cheeks. At this endearing mark of affection the French people went wild with joy, they felt sure they would have a dauphin soon! The marriage ceremony was a fairy tale, the young King looked radiant in a costume of gold brocade adorned with diamond buttons, and partly covered with a cloak of Spanish point. The Queen's ceremonial robe and cloak were of purple velvet embroidered with gold fleurs-de-lis, over the bodice an armour encrusted with precious gems shone like a myriad of stars, and on her head she wore a diamond crown locked by two fleurs-de-lis. All this was nearly forty years ago.

✤   ✤   ✤

Couchée et accouchée – couchée et accouchée – et encore couchée et accouchée[1] had been Marie Leczinska's existence for so long.

[1] To bed and produce.

Though she loved her husband with her whole being, passion had never entered into that love. In a way they both became satiated with the *couchée et accouchée* monotony. She felt relieved at the King's less frequent demands without realizing how much the first part pertained to a man's nature. The Court which had marvelled and deplored the King's faithfulness was quick to detect a certain listlessness in his demeanour: without losing an instant they searched for an attractive woman able to awake his sleeping senses. Was it by coincidence that the Comtesse de Mailly crossed his path, as it seems strange to believe that these connoisseurs should have selected her, who was neither pretty nor young? In time she really came to love the King for himself and suffered bitterly when her sister the Marquise de Vintimille treacherously ousted her from favour. The Marquise had confided to a friend when still in the convent that she would get rid of her sister and govern the King, France and all Europe. After two years of political domination she died suddenly. Immediately the Duchesse de Chateauroux, another of the Nesle sisters, appeared and held sway, but death reaped once more and the post of official mistress to the King again stood empty. Louis XV was extremely grieved at the death of Madame de Châteauroux, but his boon companion, the Duc de Richelieu, had already selected another 'Circé', Madame d'Etioles, who became the famous Marquise de Pompadour and reigned over the destiny of France until the day she was taken out of Versailles by a side door!

During those years the Queen had counted for little, except amid her own rather dowdy Court. The clever and intellectual men who surrounded her could not contrive to give it lustre, the Queen realized it, but the shameless rivalry between all these brilliant women, whose vanity, falseness and treachery contaminated the very air with their intrigues, made her withdraw deeper into the sober thinking regions where one could pay homage to God, and commune with one's self. She confided to a friend, 'I was too cold, the warm brilliant women took him away.' Her daughters, Mesdames de France, had joined her in her life of devotion and good works, their only distraction was a game of cards in the evenings. At times the King would brave the reproaches of the Queen's Court and visit his family, but these occasions became rare, the gulf between the chaste atmosphere of his wife and his irreverent surroundings had made these visits more and more embarrassing.

And now the Queen, worn out by it all, was slowly dying. She had suffered in her love, in her pride, yet she prayed for him, her beloved Louis, whom in her heart she had ever pardoned. She had even forgiven all those creatures whom she had hated at the time of their influence, but now it all seemed of little importance; serenely she was awaiting the final bidding. Madame du Deffand tells us: 'On the 3rd of March 1768 the Queen's condition had become alarming; she was administered yesterday morning. Just before it took place she asked to see the King, and speaking to him most touchingly, said: "Notwithstanding all the sins with which I have to reproach myself, I have great confidence in the mercy of God and if I have the happiness of seeing Him, the only grace that I will ask of Him will be to grant you a long life, and I feel assured that I shall obtain my request." They said that the King was so overcome that on leaving Her Majesty he was seen to wipe his eyes.'

The Queen had lingered for another three months. On the 24th of June, Monsieur Lassonne, the doctor in chief of their Majesties, whose prerogative it was, announced to the King the news of the Queen's death. The King rose from the chair in his private cabinet where he had sat awaiting the dénouement, followed the doctor into the Queen's room, approaching the bed and bending bestowed a last kiss on the cold forehead, then he asked for a detailed account of the end. The doctor did as he was bade, but suddenly became pale, swayed and fainted, the King caught him as he fell, carried him to an armchair and stood by his side, his eyes riveted on his wife's body, tears slowly covering his cheeks. As the religious personages, officials and attendants came into the chamber of death, the King left the room, still weeping profusely. For several days he mourned deeply, then sorrow lifted, and he returned discreetly to the attraction which was gradually absorbing his existence.

2

Versailles

In the eighteenth century Versailles was the focal point of the world; compared with its glamour the Courts of Europe seemed provincial, its magnificence was beyond the imagination of outsiders, but to those whose lives were part of its grandeur it seemed so natural – the splendour of the architecture, the bewildering brilliancy of the décor of the vast halls, sculptured gold and silver walls, the painted ceilings, lit by hundreds of wax tapers, the exquisite furniture with its bronze chasings, the legions of ushers, lackeys, pages in resplendent liveries standing about. There were courtiers in their full brocade habits, their waistcoats of a different hue, the entire costume heavily embroidered in gold or silver, the lace ruffles, the long embroidered hose, the pointed high-heeled shoes, with shining diamond buckles, the plumed three-cornered hats covering the white peruque, the whole attire ablaze with jewelled decorations. There were ladies in gorgeous damask robes with ample paniers which almost disappeared under the coat tails of the grand habits – obligatory for Court – the long trains mostly carried by a page. Versailles was an unforgettable pageant. Vatel tells us that it contained two thousand inhabitants.

Every moment at Court had its duties, in reality it was an existence of hard labour. The motto was – never to relax, never to look tired, never to be bored but to smile perpetually, always to be ready to make a witty retort – to look eager when attending the King's *lever*, which was one of the principal events of the day, the *grand couvert*, the solemn to and fro of His Majesty's rambles through the marbled *salons* – to follow him in the painted galleries, the gardens, the hunts, the concerts, the balls or the theatre in the evening, and then at the end of the day to attend to his *coucher*.

The courtiers would retire happy if the King had noticed them, if only by a glance. Then the next day it would all begin again. Some would rush from Paris to be in time to push themselves in the front row at the *lever* along with all the other noblemen aspiring for a smile from the Monarch.

In reality what an ordeal it must have been for Louis XV these ceremonious events morning and evening. In the morning at the time named by the Monarch, Monsieur Lebel his head valet usually would enter the room, or if His Majesty had not regained his bed that night would climb the small secret stairs, leading to the reigning mistress's apartment, and inform His Majesty tactfully of the time. Then the King would return to his own couch and the ceremonies would start. His relations would enter, followed by the medical professors, who would make a short inspection as to his health. When this was over he would stand before a wash-basin and his valets would rub him down with brushes, using hard bristled ones soaked in perfumed spirit, he would then don a long woollen gown, and one of the valets would bring him an assortment of wigs to choose from. Having made his choice, and wearing short hose and low shoes he would seat himself on his couch, the curtains around it would be drawn back and he would step down from the dais, and sit in a high chair, then the *grand lever* started. The doors were opened wide by the ushers and the crowd of privileged courtiers, pushing and cursing each other in an undertone trooped in, in silence they stood in tight rows looking at the King being dressed. Without any acknowledgement from His Majesty the vast number of courtiers, between one hundred and one hundred and fifty, stood staring at him in hopes of a passing look from their sovereign. His Majesty continued dressing, first his stockings then his shoes with high heels and large diamond buckles, his diamond studded garters, each of these articles had been passed on by Monsieur Lebel to one of the gentlemen who had been named that day for the high honour of handing them to the King. When the time came to hand the chemise it was always a moment of high tension to see who would have that distinction – but it was usually given to a prince of the royal blood. A similar ceremony took place in the evening at the *grand coucher*. Sometimes His Majesty would deign to say a few words to a courtier, then jealousies would spring up on all sides, but the lucky recipient of this favour would smile for several days.

The Court and Society believed in easy virtue, the delicate and gallant aura which surrounded adultery had become an art in France, and had made a travesty of love. Lovers and mistresses had become a recognized industry; faithfulness was decidedly *bourgeois*, virtue was not tolerated. The whole atmosphere reeked of lust; only one *raison d'être* prevailed – VICE – but vice in all its elegance and veilings. Education was a remote subject, the few academies were rarely half filled. Usually the young boy was destined by his family to enter the Court, and to strive to attract attention by his exquisite manner and perfect gallant attitude, as a means of succeeding in becoming a page of the King's Bed-chamber. It is true that he was taught the rudiments of reading and writing, and was given a very slight knowledge of history and geography, religion was stressed, but all these scholastic achieve-ments counted for little; what really mattered for his advancement was to look well on horseback, to dance gracefully, to draw the sword elegantly, to perfect the art of kissing a lady's hand, which consisted in bending low, barely touching with the lips the proffered fingers. At the age of sixteen he was supposed to enter one of the smart regiments and begin his military career. This meant that now he was his own master, and could openly lead the gay life of the capital into which he had already secretly delved.

At the early age of four or five, the daughters were sent to a convent. Generally at Fontevrault, Penthémont or Abbaye-au-Bois. These establishments were directed by nuns belonging to the highest aristocracy. In these religious communities the young girls learned the art of becoming perfect women of the world, great luxury surrounded them, they were allowed to receive friends, male or female, without supervision. The rich ones had their own apartments, their lady's-maid, often these children were married the day after their first communion. The wedding over, the bride and bridegroom would exchange a shy embrace; he would call her 'Madame', she 'Monsieur', then she would return to the nuns, *soi-disant* to finish her education, but in reality to await the time when she would become nubile. He, without any constraint, hardly conscious of possessing a wife, would return to his bachelor episodes.

The echoes from the Court with its scandals and intrigues penetrated the holy walls of these Convents. These young hearts fluttered with anticipation of what awaited their flight from the well of purity into the waters of iniquity. One certainty they carried into their new life was that they were not supposed to be faithful to their husband. A lover was *de rigueur*. The parents themselves were quite complacent, to demonstrate this, when Monsieur d'Argenson was being complimented on the charm and beauty of his very young niece, Mademoiselle de Berulle, he said smiling – 'Yes, we hope that she will be the cause of much gossip!' Another scene which is so full of the spirit of the time; a husband finding his wife in close intimacy with her lover cried out, 'What imprudence, Madame! You might have been discovered by someone else but me!' Husbands were wise and did not exact virtue which they themselves did not possess, and yet there was always between the spouses a certain respect and honour. When they met in the morning, the husband would gallantly kiss his wife's hand, and inquire concerning her health, she would ask him if he was satisfied with the chef, and if he had all he desired, so harmony reigned in the home. The children were in the hands of menials until the convent or Military Academy engulfed them. God had receded from the minds of this society, yet religious ceremonies took place with pomp and apparent fervour; they were attended by all that was great, but instead of prayer books, immoral literature was openly perused. A young woman aged twenty-two, when in the throes of death, repulsed in all consciousness a priest who had been called to her side to administer the last sacraments, saying: 'If I was not so ill I might amuse myself with all these baubles, but I have not the strength.'

Is not this one of the sad features of this libertine epoch? Notwithstanding all their faults, let us not try to take away their charm, their light-heartedness, their insouciant mode of life. The revolution came all too soon, and many of them walked up the steps of the guillotine with a smile of contempt to hide the agony of their terror.

The clergy were assuming an immense power, their wealth was becoming incalculable. By rapid degrees they were buying up the land, Abbeys, monasteries and convents were covering France. Many of the hierarchy wallowed in prodigal luxury, which often surpassed that of the Royal establishment. They did not even deign to cloak their extravagances, their mistresses presided at their ostentatious displays. Young boys of the aristocracy were being nominated Bishop or Cardinal, only to attain large incomes; most of these never knew their dioceses. Of course some still kept the Catholic faith clean, but the majority sullied it. Yet when all these rich and opulent ecclesiastics had vanished or fled, and the revolution had liquidated the rest, the faith, which had only slumbered, reappeared stronger and became once again the support of the world.

The King and his Ministers opposed all this extravaganza, but to no purpose. It is a curious phenomenon that notwithstanding his lack of moral discipline, Louis XV, *Le Rio très Chrétien*, whose Kingdom was called the eldest daughter of the Church, was intensely pious, and a great believer in its dogmas, he was a staunch enemy of the Jansénistes, of the Huguenots and the Philosophers. For him his sex life must have been a thing apart, entirely divorced from his faith.

It is a paradox that during this epoch of decadent society, France maintained and even widened her artistic lead. Against the celebrated geniuses of the previous century, names of writers like Montesquieu, Voltaire, Buffon, Diderot, J. J. Rousseau, stand out, and painters were produced like Watteau, Boucher, Greuze, Fragonard, Madame Vigée-Lebrun, whose talent depicted so vividly the vain sparkle of the period.

Four years, and yet no official mistress had been proclaimed! It was true that whispers were being exchanged in the different corners of the château, that soon all would be made clear. Somebody would be named but certainly not the low creature with whom it was said the King slept at present, no one at Court would tolerate it! Yet time was passing and the woman was still there!

3

The New Mistress

On the night of the 22nd April 1769 Versailles was agog.

At last the important question would be answered. From the guard-room to the audience chamber, from the kitchen to the attic the atmosphere seemed electrified by contradictory reports. It was said that an official mistress would be proclaimed and presented to His Majesty and the Royal Family, but fear mingled with anticipation was expressed on most countenances. Who would it be? Would it mean that France's destiny would once again be handled by a woman? By now the stirring news had spread far beyond the Palace, and crowds were assembling before the famous gates, all agog to hear about the spectacle which had not taken place for so long. Although they would see nothing of the event, the very thought of being near the scene satisfied their curiosity.

In the Galeries des Glaces, Louis XV, surrounded by his household and Court was waiting, agitated, anxious, pale, passing and repassing the line of courtiers, his arm was in a sling, only a few days before, while hunting, he had fallen from his horse and injured himself. Each time he paced before them they respectfully withdrew a few steps and quickly regained their position, frightened they might lose the view of the coming display. How majestic the King looked, how youthful. Although on the verge of openly breaking all moral rule he seemed in his impetuousness to defy all those who would dare to criticize his will. The daylight was fading; the lady was late! Little by little Versailles was becoming luminous. Lamps and lanterns were being lit, but still she had not arrived. The Duc de Choiseul ventured a sigh of relief, he was desperately against this ceremony, the Duc de Richelieu was for it, both intent on their own ends.

The New Mistress

The King's patience was giving out. The Duc de Richelieu's nose was glued to the window. The Duc de Choiseul was watching the King. His Majesty looked with angry eyes at the enormous ornamental clock on the wall. He made a sign to Choiseul, intending to tell him that the presentation would not take place, but Richelieu had perceived the coach driving into the courtyard, and with a note of triumph announced, 'Madame la Comtesse Du Barry craves the honour of being presented to His Majesty.' The doors slowly opened, and a dazzling apparition stood within them. The audience startled, gazed in utter silence. For a few seconds His Majesty closed his eyes, was it caused by the unbelievable beauty of his choice or the joy it would entail? Even Choiseul's partisans were overwhelmed by the loveliness of their opponent; as she approached, accompanied by her sponsor, the Comtesse de Bearn, and made her obeisance in three low sweeping reverences, people were awed by her poise, simple but perfectly dignified.

The Comtesse Du Barry had determined to crush all criticism and to captivate Versailles that evening by her beauty and elegance. If she succeeded it would mean victory, if she failed, she realized it would mean the end of her career. For that historical night she had chosen a gown which surpassed any as yet seen at the Court – a white tissue which clung to her figure, and over it the grand habit to be worn on such occasions. It was strewn with diamonds in profusion, forming garlands, bouquets and true lovers' knots, these were part of the gems which the King had sent her the night before. Diamonds covered her shoes, even the high heels glittered with them. Her golden hair which had to be powdered according to etiquette, had only been lightly touched, her neck, her arms, her fingers were ablaze with precious stones, but the radiance of her own beauty eclipsed all this magnificence.

The poets in rapturous tones describe her thus – 'Her blue eyes are shaded by long black eyelashes which curl upwards, her arched eyebrows of the same dark shade are so finely pencilled that they remind one of the wings of some exquisite bird. Her delicate eyelids are always partly lowered, imparting to her gaze a glint of voluptuousness. Her nose and mouth are most perfectly moulded;

her teeth so perfect pearls would look sham beside them, her skin resembles a rose leaf, floating in milk, her neck, the neck of a Greek statue, long and flexible.' The poets raise their voices in delirious admiration – 'Her bosom, her hand, her foot are unparalleled, and with it all she possesses the victory of youth. Her whole being pervades an atmosphere of sensuality, of love, of knowledge of amorous secrets.'

Many of those present had heard of her beauty by hearsay, still more had known her in her previous sordid trade, but the metamorphosis as she appeared before them that night was bewildering. She symbolized the verse which Voltaire said of her when gazing at one of her portraits – 'The original is made for the Gods.' In spite of all the splendour of that disquietening night we must leave Versailles for a while and gradually retrace the years which transformed a harlot into the most influential woman of France.

✢   ✢   ✢

On the 19th of August in the year 1743, in the parish church at the small town of Vaucouleurs, diocese of Toul, a very modest ceremony was taking place – the baptism of an illegitimate baby girl. Just three people were attending. The baptismal act was signed by all three, and thus it stood – 'Jeanne, natural daughter of Anne Becu, born 19th of August 1743, baptized the same day, Godfather Joseph Demange, Godmother Jeanne Barabin, who have signed with us. L. Gahon, Vicar of Vaucouleurs.'

As the Godfather handed the expected offering, he proposed that the party, including the *curé* should adjourn to the *marchand de vins* across the market-place and drink to the new Christian's health. Anne Becu had not felt strong enough to join the party. During the drinks Monsieur Demange, Madame Barabin and the *curé* discussed the rumour which was the talk of the small town. Who was the father? Madame Barabin assured the *curé* that it was the monk Baptiste Comard de Vaubernier, in religion Brother Ange, from the nearby monastery of Picpus. Monsieur Demange was not sure; the *curé* could not care less, he was enjoying his glass of wine – and the babe, calmed by a drop of that wine, slept.

The New Mistress

Anne Becu was a dressmaker, she was good-looking and warm-hearted. Hers was a difficult life, Vaucouleurs' society consisted of thrifty middle-class inhabitants, who thought more of hoarding their money than having a dress made by Mlle. Becu. So she was not above adding a few francs to her meagre income by accepting the homage of some local beau or passing stranger. With this rather mixed bag it was difficult to locate the male whom Jeanne could have called 'Papa'. In this milieu the little girl grew up. She was a pretty child and made much of by her mother's passing lovers. When she was four years old, Mlle. Becu brought another child into the world – a boy. Once again the registry was signed in the same manner – 'Claude, natural son of Anne Becu, born 14th February 1747.' Jeanne was delighted, but the town was scandalized. One illegitimate child could be tolerated, but a second one proved that Anne Becu had shown persistent immorality. So the inhabitants crossed the street when they perceived her; rebuffs on the verge of insults became too noticeable. Anne decided to sell her bed, her two armchairs, her cooking utensils and try her luck in the big capital. Some time before this a financier, Monsieur Billard Dumouceaux had had a passing fancy for her, had helped her and the *petite*, whom he predicted would become very pretty. On leaving for Paris he promised to remember them, but his promises remained promises! With her two children and a few parcels she travelled in the diligence to the unknown. Once there, in her loneliness she remembered Monsieur Billard Dumouceaux, and hoped that he might again be tempted. But she had lost much of her freshness, and when he received her, all his admiration was centred on the eight year old Jeanne. Turning to the mother he said: 'How lovely she is, how much lovelier she will become!' Anne understood that her charms had faded for her one-time lover, whose mistress at present was the famous Francesca. The latter required a cook, so it was arranged that Anne should enter her household. From this moment, Claude, her second child was never mentioned again in any of the biographies, so we must surmise that he had died. Francesca was pleased with the cook but more so with Jeanne and could not be separated from the child.

The latter was suddenly pitched from squalor into the utmost luxury; she never left the drawing-room, her mother never left the kitchen. The child was always on show, having compliments and praises showered on her, exalting her loveliness. She used to witness scenes between guests which were far from edifying. Francesca was a clever cultured woman, terribly quick-tempered and jealous of her power. One day she realized that Jeanne must have some kind of education. This impetuous woman decided to send the child to the convent of the Daughters of St. Aure in the Faubourg St. Marcel. The nuns' work consisted in educating young girls who were in need of protection – 'Where,' Allitz said, 'they would be taught to pray for an angel to protect them from the ever opened jaws of the lion awaiting to ensnare them.'[1] Those lines seemed a prophesy; Jeanne Becu was predestined to be drawn towards the lion's jaws, and eventually to fall a prey to his rapacity.

The change was dramatic! From extreme luxury she passed bewildered through the doors of the convent to austere simplicity. She was too stunned to cry, she stood and clenched her hands.

Soon she was transformed into a serious-looking child, her pretty clothes disappeared – she never saw them again. The uniform consisted of a black hood over the head, a band of coarse white linen tightly worn across the forehead, an unstarched blouse, a white serge skirt, and heavy calf leather shoes, tied with strings. No exuberance, no laughter, no knowledge of the outside world was allowed, but each child developed her character, her emotions, her passions, which would lead her inevitably through her future existence.

✤   ✤   ✤

Several years had passed, Jeanne was now nearing fifteen. Even under the disfiguring uniform her beauty was becoming a menace to the convent. The other girls would whisper: 'You are lovely, we wish we were like you.' Was she really so beautiful?

[1] Bibliotheque Nationale, Allitz, Tableaux, Humanité et Bienfaisance.

How could she find out? No looking glasses! The thought came to her – the kitchen – the highly polished saucepans! Yes, she was beautiful!

Jeanne Becu was to leave the convent that day. After eight years of seclusion she had outgrown the clothes which she had brought with her. Francesca had sent her a small trunk; it contained a dress, some linen, and a pair of shoes, but she was told by the Rev. Mother that when she had taken off her uniform and donned her new outfit, she was to leave at once and not show herself in worldly attire to those who had to stay behind. When Rev. Mother blessed Jeanne in farewell, her heart tightened, yes this beautiful child was doomed to fall a prey to danger.

Eight years had passed since Mademoiselle Francesca and Monsieur Billard Dumouceaux had seen their protégée. Her mother, Anne, who was now married to a Monsieur Rançon, alone had been permitted to visit her daughter. Francesca still reigned supreme, Anne was still doing the cooking, but trouble was surreptitiously brewing. Francesca objected to the continual presence in the kitchen of a so-called monk Gomard, he was a supposed relation of the monk who was named as Jeanne's father, but as Anne's cooking was so excellent, for the time being the situation was allowed to go on.

In her boudoir Francesca and Monsieur Billard Dumouceaux were soliloquizing about Jeanne. 'She may have become quite plain.' It is true that each time Anne had been visiting her, she had raved about her looks, but of course this meant nothing. A cab stopped; Francesca ran to the window but it was too late, the front door of the house had already closed. There was a knock, a young girl entered the room, made a little reverence and lifted her face to be kissed. Francesca exclaimed, 'Ah!' and Monsieur Billard Dumouceaux, 'Oh!' – but their meanings were a world apart. The former expressed a cry of jealous fear for the future, the latter one of almost delirious admiration. How lovely Jeanne was! Her long golden hair, her blush-like complexion, the look of purity which the long years in the convent had imprinted on her.

After a few words of greeting, Francesca told her bluntly that henceforth she would live in the kitchen and help her mother. Jeanne did not mind; she had forgotten what luxury was like, Monsieur Billard Dumouceaux tried to make a few objections, but a fierce look from his mistress silenced him.

Jeanne was really very lovely, and soon visitors for some reason or another would find their way below stairs. Francesca became alarmed, sensing that in the kitchen an exquisite being was blossoming, whilst in the drawing-room she herself was fading and fading. The danger was growing, it must be squashed at once. So under pretext of the assiduities of the monk for Anne Rançon she turned the whole clan out of the house.

Even during the moments of her greatest triumph Madame Du Barry remembered the terrible desolation she felt when hearing the sound of that closing door, when she stood dazed next to her mother in the street – one of the streets of Paris whose sordid secrets she would one day taste to the full. Her mother was crying, their few bundles surrounded them, the only security Jeanne had ever known had vanished. Anne kept repeating *tout est perdu*. Suddenly she remembered she had a husband, Monsieur Rançon – he had a room! So bravely they picked up their bundles and plodded towards that room.

A few days later the police reported that a young girl of about fifteen had been seen in the streets. She carried a tray on which were displayed different baubles – needles, snuff-boxes, ribbons, combs, which she was trying to sell. After observation and interrogation she was allowed to proceed, as nothing so far had aroused suspicion of improper behaviour. So Jeanne walked the dingy back alleys of the city, often just avoiding some excrement which housewives flung out of the windows when emptying their night pots, adding more filth to the already stinking mud of the lanes.

Jeanne's beauty startled the people as they passed. Soon her tray would be empty and she would return home to replenish it once more. She became accustomed to this mode of life, to be accosted by different types of men, some with a gentle compliment, others with a coarse joke. It amused her, it made her bolder, she decided to carry her tray to a better quarter of Paris. In these less gross surroundings the compliments were more enticing, more alluring. Soon her beauty was becoming known, well-dressed gentlemen in their chaises would appear, buy a yard of ribbon and glide a gold coin in its place, often an insinuating proposal would be added – it all became part of her trade. Anne was too busy seeking a situation as a cook to bother about her daughter. She, Jeanne, seemed to be doing well, so long as she was earning money, the way in which she was doing it did not matter much. Of course she must be careful – a brat might complicate matters! Many years later the Comte de Genlis told the Comte d'Allonville of his astonishment when he was presented to the Du Barry at Versailles, and recognized in her the beauty whom one evening his valet had brought to him, but he had sent her away – she was too young.

One day a brother of her *soi-disant* father, also a monk, discovered her. He was shocked at the way she was earning her living and assured Anne he could really help her. He happened to be chaplain to a Madame de La Garde, a rich woman whose only pleasure was to display her wealth in entertaining lavishly in her beautiful château. She loved youth, and when she was told by her chaplain of Jeanne's charm, apparent purity and innocence, she sent for her, and engaged her to become a kind of lady's maid. From the rough life in the rough uneven streets, Jeanne found undreamt-of comfort. Madame de la Garde was enchanted with her, even during some of her greatest receptions she would send for Jeanne to show off her loveliness. Accustomed to admiration . . . and more . . . the young girl did not abstain from responding, Madame de la Garde soon perceived that Jeanne's innocence did not resist too deeply to temptation, so the lovely child was once again cast out, and brutally propelled into the repellent hardship of her mother's two rooms.

✣   ✣   ✣

In 1760 Jeanne was eighteen and divinely beautiful. Whilst she sat mending the holes in her one dress – she had had to leave behind the fashionable clothes which Madame de la Garde had provided for her, a strong feeling of resentment overcame her. She could not go on leading this life; surely a brilliant destiny awaited her! The men whom she allowed to teach her the way of love had only pointed the way to her career! She must be seen, she must be known.

At that time the shops in the renowned city of Paris were only dark hovels with wooden shutters, half opened to allow the passers-by to get a glimpse at the objects for sale. There was little choice, but as there was no comparison people still enjoyed peeping in. Over each façade hung a board indicating the trade of the merchant, the latter usually slept at the back of this uninviting abode, a peephole in the door enabled him to watch for thieves. A few years later better shops appeared in the Rue St. Honoré. Slowly they extended to some of the adjoining streets, by degrees they had become more elegant and more luxurious; glass frontages allowed a view of the fascinating articles and also of the attractive shopgirls. Leclerc in his suite, Costumes d'Esnault & Rapilly, describes the costume of these enticing demoiselles.

A dress in muslin trimmed with furbelows, the slender waist elongated by a bodice ending in a point; on their heads a large black satin hood, which allowed their golden locks to escape in profusion; dainty shoes with high heels and silver buckles, in their hands they held small flimsy fans which they fluttered as they strutted along. These girls hovered from counter to counter mesmerizing the men to buy the most extravagant and needless articles. The masculine element outnumbered the feminine customers. The handsome marquis in his satin coat, the important and solemn financier, the flippant officer of the Garde Française, and the Petits Abbés with their affected phraseology and prancing on their red heels, would playfully help the laughing sales girls to measure the lace they had purchased. On entering this domain, one was immediately enveloped in a gentle amorous atmosphere, many *billet-doux* passed from hand to hand. It was not an easy game, the *patron* was severe and the one condition he insisted upon when engaging his staff was that none was allowed out at night. The girls slept in one long dormitory, so could be easily

Louis XV by Louis-Michel Van Loo

Marie Leczinska by Nattier

supervised, only on Sundays were they free, so all the fun and love had to be enjoyed on that day.

Among these shops in the Rue Neuve-des-Petits-Champs was *A la Toilette*, owned by Monsieur Labille, the incomparable *modiste*. People would stop for hours gazing in at the wonderful decorations, at the gay boxes of flowers, at the high-born ladies who honoured Monsieur Labille's with their custom, and at the *demi-mondaines* who did likewise and who in those days consisted mostly of the theatre world.

In her anxiety to start her future Jeanne resolved to enter this establishment and join the seraglio of youth. She borrowed a friend's dress and presented herself to Monsieur Labille. Needless to say there was no hesitation in engaging her, and Jeanne was to enter his establishment the next day. She had to confess that she possessed no clothes, he told her that this was of no consequence and gave orders that she should be given an entire trousseau. The following morning as she appeared among the cluster of her future companions, there was a stir and a murmur of '*Quelle beauté*'.

Each Sunday morning the swarm of pretty *midinettes* would step out of their dormitory, free until ten o'clock at night, looking like Fragonard figures in their feastday clothes of ivory cotton cloth with ample blue paniers, folded across their small exquisitely formed bosoms a muslin fichu in which often nestled a pink rose, and poised on their high coiffures a small flowered hat, slanting towards their saucy eyes.

Jeanne looking demure would first pay a visit to her mother, but this would be short, she knew someone was waiting for her. She and he would meet, and hand in hand find their way to the fair of St. Germain, or the more exclusive one of St. Cloud, this turbulent fête which the pictures of the time bring to us, the marionettes, the Pierrots and Columbines. Later the simple collation near the Fountain under the green arcades, the sound of laughter and song which seemed to ricochet from tree to tree, permeating the air. When the supreme moment of the whole day would draw near, still hand in hand they reached the haven where she and he would lose themselves in ecstasy. Much later, in the virtuous dormitory of Monsieur Labille, Jeanne would lay awake reliving the hours she had spent in the arms of the man who appealed to her for the moment.

For some months Jeanne's life varied little, for her the only break in the monotony consisted in changing her paramours. None up to now had seemed of any consequence: and through her apparent frivolity and sensuality she kept a level head. Whenever she became aware that a serious liaison was in sight she gracefully dismissed the disillusioned male.

Notwithstanding the difficulties of avoiding Monsieur Labille's strict rule, a slight scandal occurred about this time, a young hairdresser named Lametz became another of Jeanne's victims. It was said that they had been living together for four months when it happened. He was supposed to be teaching her the art of hairdressing, but after a time his mother became suspicious and soon discovered that teaching hair style was the least of his occupations at the Rançons' home, so in a fury she went there and upbraided them in the most abusive language, calling them the lowest prostitutes in Paris, trying to induce her son to marry that strumpet of a daughter. Madame Rançon complained to the police who strictly forbade Madame Lametz to go near them, but the neighbours missed none of the scene, and soon the story spread. The young man, ruined by Jeanne's excessive extravagances, fled to England.

When Jeanne was twenty, it seemed as if the real purpose or motif of her destiny dawned, slowly to creep to the height of fame, only to precipitate itself under the agonizing knife of the revolution. Anne Rançon rarely interfered in her daughter's life, but one Sunday morning when Jeanne arrived to give her mother the usual weekly kiss, Anne was stirred by the enchantment of her child's radiance, she exclaimed, 'You are so lovely, my Jeannette, your figure is utter perfection, and that is the greatest attraction to men, you must stop losing your time with all these insignificant wastrels, you must reflect and establish your future with a serious liaison.' Jeanne was quite willing!

Madame Rançon had been told by a neighbour that there was a certain Madame Duquesnoy who kept a famous gambling house,

The New Mistress

which was frequented by the highest names in society, by millionaires for whom money did not count, who besides the games, were known for their mode of life and ready to squander their gold on lewdness. So Jeanne said farewell to Monsieur Labille and prepared herself for serious pursuit of sin. Madame Duquesnoy owned a fine mansion in the Rue de Bourbon, where she entertained lavishly the different worlds of Paris, men crowded there to lose money and to search for a new feminine distraction, women went there to offer themselves for the distraction, high gambling veiled the sex question, while the sex question veiled the high gambling.

The night Jeanne made her début in this paradise of iniquity was noted by Madame Duquesnoy as one of her most successful evenings. Once again as so often before, the guests stood abashed by such a harmonious miracle of the flesh. Among the staring crowd a man disentangled himself from a group and with assurance spoke to her, Jeanne responded, they were no novices of this procedure – 'I am Comte Du Barry.' 'I am Jeanne Vaubernier,' thus they became acquainted. In this assembly of high distinguished debauchery, Jeanne felt that she was far from being their equal, there was a certain refinement in their approach which she had not yet encountered; in the world she had lived in, men were either amorously brutal or vulgarly sloppy. In her bewilderment she spoke to her mother – 'I felt a peasant, they are so graceful.' Anne encouraged her daughter – 'You will quickly learn their bows and nothingness, learn it all but remain yourself, men tire of always eating capons and delicate fruit; a good cabbage now and then delights them.' When Jeanne mentioned Du Barry Anne became excited, 'The Comte Du Barry, don't lose sight of him, who knows? He may become a stepping stone.'

A few days later Jeanne entered the Comte Du Barry's gates, in reality she never escaped from their bars. She did not care for him, he cared less, but when gazing at her that evening at Madame Duquesnoy's, he knew that his great ambition might be fulfilled and that Louis XV would once again have an official mistress, and he would be the provider.

23

Comte Jean Du Barry was good looking, he originated from Toulouse, of decent family, but he himself was an adventurer. Up to the age of twenty-eight he had lived in his native town squandering the greater part of his important fortune on gambling, women and ribaldry, he then realized that Toulouse was provincial and his reputation rather shady; in Paris he might work up a new social position and obtain an entrée to some political or diplomatic post – so he set forth to the capital. After many rebuffs he secured through one of the Ministers an interest in divers operations, which allowed him to rebuild part of his income. He augmented his revenue by expedients of a doubtful character, and lived in extravagance and in a brilliant entourage, but this ostentation had a definite object in view – his aspiration was to become important by procuring a successor to Madame de Pompadour. In a way this was known and earned him the name 'Cad', but still people forgot all this when drinking his excellent wines and eating the best of food.

Although no one guessed the depth of the working of Du Barry's mind, people were not gullible. They gave him credit for procuring their amusement and avoiding open scandal. He, for his part, never allowed an opportunity to slip by, seemingly unconcerned, like a spider he watched for a victim to ensnare in his web. The graceful girls and attractive women who filled his drawing-rooms were all for sale, most of them he had discovered during his travels; some were rather raw; others were already acutely shrewd. He tested their reactions and with those worthy of the future he had destined for them, he took infinite trouble to educate, polish and fashion them until perfection was attained, the others he sent home. Then the chosen ones appeared, ready for friend or foe, but never would they be allowed to escape from his power, even when far away he would continue to direct their lives for his own benefit in whatever manner he wished. This was the man with whom Jeanne was to start her dream of a serious liaison.

4

Madame Du Barry

On the 14th of December 1764 the Inspector of Police reported –
'The current mistress of the Comte Du Barry is a striking young
woman aged about nineteen, tall, well proportioned and noble
looking, named Mlle. Vaubernier. They appeared together in a
box at the Théâtre des Italiens.'[1] A few nights later she attended
the ball of the Opéra, clothed entirely in white. Monsieur
d'Espinchal, one of the critics of the time who was there, wrote in
his manuscripts, 'I have never in my life seen a more agreeable
vision than this celestial figure, it was Hébé, it was one of the
Graces, Voltaire's poem concerning Agnès Sorel would have
fitted her perfectly.'[2]

> 'Jamais l'Amour ne forma rien de tel:
> Elle avait tout, elle aurait dans ses chaines,
> Mis les heros, les sages et les rois.'

> 'Never before had love created such perfection,
> And bestowed on her so much grace,
> She would have ensnared heroes, Kings and sages.'

Jean Du Barry realized that if his aim was to be achieved, only a
complete upheaval of his present way of life could bring a spark of
respectability to his nickname the 'Cad'.

Jeanne now presided at the head of his table at Rue de la
Jussienne with all his numerous servants at her command. She
kept open house to Du Barry's guests, her sole duty was to be-
witch men. By now most of the females for sale had disappeared,
only a few had been allowed to remain, to decorate the scene.

[1] *Journal de Monsieur Sartines*, cité par Mr. Vatel, Tome 1, page 81.
[2] *Manuscrit d'Espinchal*, Bibliothèque, Clermont Ferrand.

Anne Rançon was asked to come and supervise the household staff, once more she remained below stairs while her daughter feasted in the upper floors – as for poor Monsieur Rançon, nobody knew or cared where he slept. Jean Du Barry eliminated from his circle all those whose ancestry was slightly vague, and in these highly respectable new conditions he launched into the artistic world.

From then on his receptions glittered with well-known poets, intellectuals and courtiers, amongst these such grand seigneurs as the Duc de Duras and the Duc de Richelieu. Now the advice of Anne to her daughter 'Learn their bows and their nothingness, but remain yourself,' floated in Jeanne's brain, she was determined to follow the counsel. The Duc de Richelieu, who had no illusions concerning Jean Du Barry's morals, nevertheless liked him. One day they were discussing the King's dissolute mode of life, a danger to his health, saying the pavilion in the Parc-aux-Cerfs at Versailles had virtually become a brothel. Nearly every night his valet Lebel, or one of the gentlemen of the same feather, would procure some young female for the King's pleasure, he would go there, sample her and have her taken away; if only he could be induced to take a proper mistress! Du Barry leaped with excitement – 'Mon cher Monsieur le Duc, we have the very jewel with which to dazzle His Majesty – Mlle. Vaubernier.' The Duc stared at Du Barry, then struck by the enormity of the proposal, went into a paroxysm of laughter, 'My good friend, have you lost all sense of humour? Do you see Choiseul, Mesdames and the Dauphin's faces? It is the funniest joke I have heard for years.' Still doubled with laughter, Richelieu dismissed Du Barry. When walking down the monumental staircase, the echo of mirth followed Jean, but all the same he felt that the idea had been launched.

Notwithstanding all the rumours concerning the King's scandalous behaviour at Le Parc-aux-Cerfs, where it was said bacchanalian orgies were perpetrated, the people of France loved Louis XV. They referred to him as 'The Beloved'. He was their anointed Monarch, surrounded by glory, which to them made him immortal. At Court perhaps the veneration was less crude, but the outward result was just as servile.

Jeanne was learning to become a woman of society – of a certain society which comprised making the acquaintance of *demi-mondaines*. Amongst them she was introduced to the well-known Mlle. Legrand, the literary blue-stocking and hostess of the period, whose *salon* was a meeting place for the great brains of the time. Jeanne listened attentively to the assault of wit, the brilliant repartees, where the most audacious questions were discussed without a shadow of shame.

By now Jean Du Barry had become too absorbed in scheming Jeanne's future into the Royal couch to mind about her mode of life. Their mild attraction for one another had waned, up to a point her body was her own, with the exception that before taking her pleasure her passing whim should be medically declared free from contagious disease. His Majesty must be safeguarded!

Monsieur Lebel, the King's head valet, was a necessary personage to approach. He was the key accessory to his master plan. He was very close to the Monarch's heart since the King relied on his skill and devotion to cloak his many indiscretions, so Jean determined to make the acquaintance of this most important gentleman.

Du Barry's consistent allusion to Jeanne as 'A King's morsel' had begun to bear fruit with the Duc de Richelieu; he now seemed to assimilate the possible meeting of His Majesty Louis XV with Jeanne Vaubernier, who had now taken the name of Comtesse Du Barry. Jean asked the Duc to introduce him to Lebel, and suggested he should bring him to a small dinner-party at his house, and view his pictures. Monsieur Lebel did not seem enamoured by this proposal, as Du Barry's shady reputation had preceded him; he was loath to mix in this nefarious milieu. Yet after a time, under the Duc's pressure, Lebel yielded and a date was arranged. Although no mention of Jeanne had been made, she was the first to greet him when he entered the reception room. He was taken aback, she looked too perfect to be of this world, all in white – she mostly wore white – her beautiful hair barely powdered, it seemed as if gold dust had been scattered on that lovely head. The dinner was exquisite, the wines perfect and the hostess eclipsed all the pictures he had admired earlier on in Jean's gallery. Besides being dazzled by her features he was enjoying her conversation, her anecdotes, not always in the best of taste, but told without the least embarrassment or pretension. 'Yes! THE KING MUST SEE HER.'

Lately His Majesty had mentioned the word 'Boredom'. The nightly strolls to the Parc-aux-Cerfs were becoming monotonous, the successive bouquets of females less and less exciting, Lebel realized that for a time Jeanne might revive and titillate his jaded senses. A few evenings later, when he was attending to the Monarch prior to the *débotté* His Royal Master yawned and said, 'Lebel my good friend, I have enough of your damsels, you can close the Parc-aux-Cerfs for a time.' Feeling that this was the chosen moment, Lebel broke forth with enthusiasm, 'Sire, two nights ago a woman who seemed to belong to the immortals crossed my life. No words would be adequate to describe such seduction, such perfection, such simplicity, she might amuse Your Majesty for a while. I could arrange a meeting where Your Majesty could see her, whilst being entirely protected from view.' The King relying on Lebel, consented to his scheme, and faced the *grand coucher* in a less bored manner.

In the artistic dining-room of Monsieur Lebel in Versailles, a gay dinner-party was assembled. Only a few people were sitting around the exquisitely-laid table, the Duc de Richelieu, the Duc de Duras, the Comte Du Barry, the host, Monsieur Lebel and Jeanne. The wine was flowing, the dishes were irreproachable, wit, and laughter rocked the air. Jeanne was brilliant, the wines had made her less careful of decorum, it had flushed her, she felt elated in this exclusively male gathering. Her dress had slipped from her bare shoulders uncovering part of her bosom and as she clinked glasses, her sparkling eyes cast voluptuous glances over each one present. Unknown to her, from a peep hole in the wall the King watched!

Lebel was anxious, he could no longer refrain from ascertaining the King's impressions about what he had just seen, so with a muttered excuse he left his guests. His Majesty was waiting, he seemed agitated, as he perceived his valet, he exclaimed, 'She is divine, I must talk to her at once; arrange a meeting.' Lebel tried to expostulate, 'But Sire, the *grand coucher* is already late, may I suggest postponing the introduction until tomorrow.' 'No, Lebel, put off the ceremony, I must see her again in your private rooms.'

It was long past midnight, Lebel's guests had left, only Jeanne remained. Lebel was hesitating, the thought of the King awaiting his call made him nervous. Somewhere he could hear people walking about, doubtless his lackeys clearing the remains of the party downstairs, he must tarry a while. Jeanne was dozing peacefully, she had been told what to expect, for her it was nothing new! At last no more sound, the servants must have retired, to make sure he visited the apartments below – yes – no one, then he called to Jeanne – 'I am going to bring the King.' That night Jeanne treated the King as she had treated scores of her lovers. She did not feign innocence or embarrassment at the honour conferred on her, she was simply herself: tender, revealing to him the secrets of her trade. Louis had never encountered such a being; beautiful, voluptuous and yet possessing the artlessness of an adolescent!

On account of Mesdames and the Dauphin Jeanne's nocturnal visits were veiled in secrecy, only Lebel knew the hour she arrived at night and the early one at which she left at dawn. The King was driven almost insane by his passion, uncontrollable fits of temper and sudden incomprehensible outbursts of laughter bewildered his entourage. Lebel was frightened, his little joke of titillating the King's appetite was a joke no longer, a whole week had passed, and he was still bringing Jeanne to His Majesty. Whom could he consult, who would share his anxiety? The only person he could trust and who knew the position was the Duc de Richelieu, after all he was the promoter of Du Barry's scheme. The Duc, who had not heard the latest detail, received Lebel with trepidation, Lebel followed the Duc into his private cabinet, Richelieu handed him his snuff-box, but Lebel fumbled, his hand shook, he could hardly hold the pinch of snuff.

'Monsieur le Duc I have come to ask your help. The King will kill himself unless he ceases this game. I have misled His Majesty at the start, telling him that the Vaubernier was married and of noble birth. I said this to allay his conscience.'

Richelieu seemed amazed, he reflected for a few seconds, then retorted, 'But, *mon ami*, I see no remedy unless you tell him that you have lied and that she is not married, and working under a false name.'

'But,' shouted Lebel, losing all control in his fear, 'His Majesty will never trust me again.'

Richelieu approached his visitor and rejoined, 'If you don't, I will, since I do not relish the thought of having to adopt a respectful attitude before Jeanne Vaubernier in the future.'

That afternoon when Lebel entered the King's cabinet to attend to him His Majesty was sitting at a large table, his head buried between his hands, he did not move or look to see who had entered, guessing it was Lebel, he murmured, 'I am so tired my friend, and yet I cannot keep away from her.' As the Monarch lifted his eyes towards him, Lebel sensed the moral agony his master was suffering, there was no time to lose; the King was wasting his strength on that creature, he must speak.

'Sire, I have lied to you, the Comtesse Du Barry is neither noble nor married, in fact,' Lebel continued, 'she is Du Barry's mistress and is known to have an appalling background. The gendarmes are well acquainted with her past. In fact, Sire, she is a whore.'

Louis XV without the least tremor said casually, 'Find her a convenient husband and after the marriage bring her to Compiègne.'

Lebel felt the tragedy of the King's decision, if the unsavoury details concerning the lady's life, which he had just exposed without restraint, did not alter the position, he knew that a prostitute was on the verge of becoming the first lady of France.

In his wretchedness Lebel still hoped that a way might be found
to prevent the disaster which he had provoked, he still held a card
in his hand – 'The Cad' – but he soon discovered that the latter
held the whole pack. Feigning to condole with the one who
solicited his help, Du Barry said, 'Perhaps it would solve the
whole episode if Jeanne married, it would be easier to stop the
liaison from becoming official. I have a brother who lives in the
country and is badly off, he is a simple creature and will be only
too happy to oblige us, of course I will tell him the condition
directly the ceremony is over, and he should receive for this
service a handsome sum. After that he would disappear.'

Not even waiting for his brother's answer, Jean Du Barry
decided to start the delicate task of instructing Jeanne in the
manner she was to accept as true the lies and inventions he was
devising to establish her high ancestry. His imagination was running riot. For the King's sake his official mistress must have a
status which could vie with many of the court ladies, yet to transform Anne Becu from a peasant into a high and mighty lady
required tact and ingenuity. First a birth certificate must be
fabricated for Jeanne. A trustworthy friend was sent to Vaucouleurs, and with a little skill and a few bribes, Jeanne became the
legitimate daughter of Jean-Baptiste Gomard de Vaubernier and
Anne Becu, as for her humble godparents, Joseph Demange and
Barabin, they were given handles to their names, and emerged as
Joseph de Mange and Dame Jeanne de Barabin. The forgery went
still further, making the date of birth 1746 instead of 1743.

Louis XV was becoming impatient and expressed his surprise
and annoyance that the marriage had not yet taken place. Alas, a
great loss had occurred for the King; his most trusted valet and
friend Lebel had died. So many plans had been retarded! His
intimate friend had declared that the Du Barry affair had pre-
cipitated his death. The King had grieved and had even had a mass
said for his valet's soul, but as Louis's life now attained a new and
overwhelming interest, all else seemed of small value.

·   ·   ·   ·   ·

At last all was ready to transform Jeanne, the new aristocrat of ancient lineage, to the bewildering titles and noble status of the Du Barrys. On the 1st of September 1768 at five o'clock in the morning, in the chilly and dimly lit Church of St. Laurent, the marriage took place. At 5.30 the bridegroom with a low bow to his wife walked slowly out of the edifice, and was seen no more. At 10.30 His Majesty was informed in Compiègne. Jeanne Becu's title was now truly hers.

The wily Jean Du Barry foresaw the difficulties which would arise at the beginning of Jeanne's new role on the boards of the most fastidious and critical stage of the world – THE COURT OF FRANCE. His genius was immediately revealed. In a way, all that Louis XV loved in Jeanne must be tactfully softened, the wild unrestrained nature in Jeanne must be subdued and yet not crushed. It was necessary to shield her from ridicule, the greatest calamity which could befall anyone. She must be guarded against blunders, from indulging in cheeky remarks, from resorting to coarse jokes, from making mocking grimaces, she must learn to stem the joys and the tears, the small occasional fits of anger, in fact the very essence on which the life of a dissolute woman is built. Jeanne was quick to notice the reaction of the courtiers when she first appeared at Versailles, and the mocking remarks which were uttered behind ornate fans.

Jeanne Vaubernier was now a respectable married woman. Although not entitled to certain honours until the day she would be officially presented to the King, she could show herself openly and reside under the same roof as her lover.

The King was at Compiègne with the Court; his daughters were also in residence at the château. He sent for Jeanne, this was the first time she would appear as the King's mistress. Out of discretion Louis felt it would give less licence to gossip if he took a house in the town for Jeanne. Jean Du Barry decided that the Comtesse Du Barry should impress the Court by her dazzling way of life. She arrived at Compiègne preceded and followed by a retinue of lackeys in brilliant liveries, of lady's maids, of chefs, of horses and carriages, and installed herself in her new abode. She met the King only when she was alone. Choiseul in his memoirs describes his arrival at Compiègne and his conversation with Monsieur St. Florentin: '. . . nobody is quite sure who she is, but there is a lady in this town, with an enormous staff and living in the greatest luxury, she sleeps with the King every night.' At once Choiseul fathomed that the 'thing' against which he had been fighting had actually come to pass. The scandal was growing and indignation was fanned by all around. After a while Louis XV left for Fontainebleau. People were wondering what would become of the Du Barry, perhaps it was a way of breaking off with her. Mesdames felt that the château was too historical to desecrate its rooms with a street walker, but to the astonishment of all, behold, a few days later after the King's arrival, a noisy clatter in the courtyard made everyone run to the windows, and there in all her splendour Jeanne stepped out from her coach. She was assigned a handsome apartment, near the King.

The Empress Marie-Theresa of Austria kept in constant correspondence with her envoy, Count Mercy-D'Argenteau. She was anxious to ascertain the state of affairs at Court as her daughter, Marie Antoinette, was destined to become the young Dauphin's wife. The Ambassador reported, 'The King's mistress lives in the apartments described as the *cour des femmes*, which is easily accessible to the King, she is surrounded by great luxury and a regiment of servants whose liveries rival the royal ones. The lady does not appear in the Royal Chapel, as she is still not presented officially, so a Chapel has been installed for her private use below the banqueting Hall. She seems to accept all the grandeur as if she had been born a Cleopatra, the Court does not relish this state of affairs.'

Now the only barrier to the Comtesse Guillaume Du Barry's final triumph was that as yet she had not been publicly acknowledged as the King's mistress; that meant being presented officially to the King and the Royal Family. Even Louis realized it would require a genius to push it through. The opposition grew fierce, the Duc de Choiseul declared it was an impossibility. His sister the

Duchesse de Grammont was adamant, since to the Duchesse the Du Barry was the usurper who had ousted her from the coveted position of the King's favourite. She declared that there would be an exodus of the ladies around His Majesty if that street walker was publicly acknowledged. It was a rebellion! But this concerted opposition of the nobility made the King all the more determined to have Jeanne definitely established, his only hesitation arose from the dreaded *vox populi*.

On the other hand, Jean Du Barry was spurring on Jeanne to take her rightful place at Court; this would give her the prerogatives of travelling in the King's coach, of appearing at banquets, and of attending Mass in the Royal Chapels. Sensing that this moment might be the turning point of the whole edifice, Jean Du Barry told Jeanne to stage a scene with the King, and to threaten that unless she was publicly recognized as his mistress she would leave him and never return.

Exhausted by all this wrangling, the King told Jeanne – 'Well, find yourself a sponsor.' A lady of high rank always accompanied the person to be presented at the ceremony, she was supposed to introduce her to the Monarch. That posed another problem!

A chase started, since nobody would accept such a task, there was a limit, they said, to lowering oneself. The situation was becoming alarming, when a ray of hope occurred. The Baronne de Montmorency, of rather shady reputation, said she might consider sponsoring the Comtesse Du Barry, if she were adequately compensated for the ordeal, the sum she mentioned staggered the Treasury, her good services were declined. Several more shady comtesses and a rather broken down marquise were approached, but nearly all demanded a million or so of livres, in addition to this, one demanded to be given the title of Duchesse. At last Richelieu, who unbeknown to anyone had been trying to unearth a victim, discovered that a certain Comtesse de Bearn, an addict to gambling, was living in poverty and crippled with debts, which she was unable to meet. When she was asked if she would act as sponsor, she was delighted to accept. The sum she was to receive was two hundred thousand livres and the gown which she would wear on the occasion.

Louis' pride was deeply hurt by the insult to his position, in that none save an ostracized old gambling hag had deigned to accept the choice he had made of a companion.

Jeanne was now living in the Château de Versailles. She occupied Lebel's apartment, she had brought with her all the grandeur and elegance which she possessed, and toyed with them as if her whole existence had been one long time of refinement, behaving always as if immorality had never touched her. The growing animosity against her was becoming a menace. Choiseul and the Duchesse de Grammont were gathering followers, Jeanne knew it, but she was waiting for her revenge when she would act.

Libels, ridiculing episodes were being circulated, lies and atrocious anecdotes began to appear, her name scarcely veiled.

> 'Quelle merveille!
> Une fille de rien,
> Quelle merveille!
> Donne au Roi de l'Amour.
> Est à la Cour.

> Vous distinguez, je crois, celle qu'à notre Cour
> On soutenait n'avoir jamais été cruelle. . . .
> Qui dans Paris ne connut ses appas?
> Du laquais au Marquis chacun se souvient d'elle.'

> 'What a marvel to see at Court,
> A girl of nothing, making love to its Lord.

> 'I think we all notice at Court,
> She who was generous and fair with her wares,
> Since in Paris from lackey to Marquis,
> All could buy their share!'

35

Choiseul was ruthless in his determination to chase her out of sight; in his strength he knew that nothing could withstand his power. The King was beginning to realize that he alone clung to his mistress, and that the whole of France was turning away with disgust. It pained him. Even last evening his daughters had asked to be received privately. He had feared their visit, would it concern Jeanne? To his astonishment, when they had kissed his hand, Madame Adelaide spoke:

'We have come, dear Papa, to implore you to hear our request with patience and condescension, we feel that the country demands a Queen; you are still young and likely with God's will to reign over us all for years to come. For two weeks we have been making novenas to bring us light, and we agree with the country. Our choice has fallen on the Archduchess Elizabeth of Austria, the sister of Marie Antoinette, we have taken much information and are told that she is good and charming, very intelligent and beautifully educated, and although she is young, she is capable in every manner of becoming "Reine de France".'

Louis was sitting in an armchair; he rose, Mesdames stood before him. Deep down in his heart he knew they were right, the same thought had come to him, but what of Jeanne? He would have to renounce all connection with her. The pain grew stronger, he knew that he would cease to exist should she leave him, and yet he could not brutally tell his children that he was so entangled in his sinful life that he had lost the moral strength to break the net which had now ensnared his very soul, so with his captivating smile he became a very tender Papa and said:

'My darling daughters I must think over your solicitude for me and our country. Of course in view of my age, the young Archduchess might hesitate, first of all we must ascertain her reaction to the idea. Should she be willing, I shall send my painter Ducreux to make a portrait of her and Marie Antoinette, then we could suggest my going to visit Austria.'

The rather dowdy women once again curtseyed low, kissed their father's hand and left him alone, Louis sighed with relief and took out of his inner pocket a miniature of Jeanne, pressed it to

Madame Du Barry, print of the time

Banquet offered by the Comtesse Du Barry to Louis XV on the completion of the Château de Louveciennes by Moreau le jeune

his lips and whispered, 'Never shall we part until death separates us,' then taking his quill pen he wrote those words at the back of its diamond frame. In time Ducreux returned from Austria. The portraits were enchanting, but Louis refused to become the brother-in-law of his grandson, the Dauphin, later Louis XVI, whose betrothal to Marie Antoinette was going to be announced.

The Duc de Choiseul had prompted Mesdames to approach their father in their great distress. They passed their days in prayer imploring God to deter him from another example of degradation. Now the last hope had vanished, for it would remind them, as it did four years ago, of the King's utter disdain for the law of Christian faith. Was it superstition or a spark of deep faith which made the King find some new pretext to postpone the event of the presentation?

The Duc de Richelieu felt that now or never must the presentation take place. The whole of France was taking part, even in the distant provinces it was becoming a bone of contention. He asked to be received by the King.

'Sire,' he told him, 'every detail for the ceremony is definitely in order. The Comtesse Du Barry's sumptuous trousseau is complete, her future apartments are awaiting her. She will move into Madame Adelaide's abode, from which a secret stairway leads to your Majesty's rooms, her staff has been augmented, her stables are filled, coaches and the enchanting sedan chair have been redecorated with the arms and coronets of the Du Barrys. They are the ones which belonged to the Marquise de Pompadour. I believe, Sire, that to postpone the ceremony might bring trouble; once it has taken place, all mouths will be closed.'

His Majesty still seemed uncertain, but said, 'I shall fix the date tonight.'

That night Louis told Richelieu, 'The presentation will take place on the 22nd of April.'

5

'Queen of Shame'

For twenty-six years we have travelled back into the past, today, the 22nd of April 1769, we are once again gazing on the Comtesse Du Barry, who has just been proclaimed the official mistress of Louis XV, King of France. She has performed all that etiquette required and has been received by the Dauphin, she has penetrated the gloomy atmosphere of Mesdames de France, Madame de Bearn has received her promised bribe and left. Jeanne has returned to her apartment, the courage which had sustained her during all these hours seemed to leave her and she sobbed. That night Louis came to her late.

The next day, Sunday, 23rd of April, in the ornate Chapel of the Château de Versailles, the King's Mass was about to start, every possible prie-dieu was occupied, the galleries were overflowing with courtiers, they had all come eager to witness a scene of sacrilege. Many Bishops were surrounding the celebrant, Choiseul was there, there was a stir, Mesdames and the Dauphin made their entrance. The assembly stood in respect, then after a certain interval Madame Du Barry, covered in diamonds, appeared, and took her seat in the tribune – so long occupied by Madame de Pompadour. Lastly the King entered the crowded chapel – he looked agitated, all again stood. The King glanced at his mistress with a half smile, the priest intoned the Mass – '*In nomine patris*', the Monarch made the sign of the Cross, the Du Barry imitated him and both bowed down to adore the Creator, the assembly stared. The Mass ended, the *curé* had offered it for Marie Leczinska. That evening Jeanne Du Barry attended the concert given by the Dauphin and Mesdames.

A little time before the presentation Jean Du Barry had obtained the King's permission to nominate one of his sisters to be a sort of companion and adviser to Jeanne. They called her 'Chon', short for Franchon. She was far from being good-looking, was slightly hunchbacked and walked with a limp, but she was agreeable, clever and shrewd. The King had felt greatly relieved at this suggestion. Piercing through his passion was the apprehension of Jeanne's contact with his entourage. Jean Du Barry having thus secured a strong foothold over his former mistress, had kept away from the crowded Court. He judged that behind the scenes he could better grasp the situation and gauge the effect Jeanne was creating at Versailles. As well as placing by her side a mentor worthy of himself he had devised a way of communicating with Jeanne by means of a band of young men who rode incessantly between Paris and Versailles to bring her messages as to her behaviour, questions and answers. Yet with all these precautions, whilst sitting at the King's whist table, Jeanne had not hesitated to say to the King in a loud voice, 'You are the greatest liar in the world!' On another occasion while drinking coffee at a banquet, Louis XV had poured some down his habit; Jeanne, reverting to her old ways, shouted, *'France, ton café fout le camp!'* The King was greatly amused, but eyes around him were lifted in disgust. One evening at her card table she played a wrong card and said, 'I am fried!' – meaning I have lost, a sharp-tongued onlooker said, 'But Madame you must be used to that' – alluding to her mother when a cook with Francesca.[1] Mademoiselle Chon would try to modify her language, but the words which Jeanne had lived with were hard to kill. Still under Chon's constant direction they became rarer and fainter, yet they never quite lost their grip.

Although an apt pupil, Chon often despaired of turning Jeanne into a *grande dame*. Some days suddenly Jeanne would break into one of her ballads, throw off her fine clothes and in her lovely nakedness belong once again to the time of freedom. Chon would try to coax her back to decorum, but Jeanne would cry out:

'I am utterly fed up with all this mimicry and stupid manners, I hate them all – those noble trollops, hiding behind their titles and

[1] Edmond et Jules de Goncout – *La Du Barry*.

shamelessly stealing the bread of us prostitutes. I often think it is not worth it all. I know for sure that if anything happens to Louis I shall be thrown out, too worn out to resume my old trade, and I shall die of hunger.'

At this outburst of rebellion, Chon would leave her, she understood the strain this girl was going through and she herself often wondered if it was worthwhile. Yet when the hour to reappear would chime, Jeanne would emerge, gowned and bejewelled so as to dominate all others, her head upright, her knees almost unable to support her, her heart filled with dread at the thought of the insulting looks she would encounter as she walked alone into those rooms full of antagonism.

✤   ✤   ✤

The dominating attitude of Jean Du Barry was becoming intolerable, and Jeanne resolved that as soon as she felt her position secure, she would eliminate him from her life. She loathed him, he loathed her, since he knew that the moment she realized her power, his game would be up; but until the evil day arrived he would have managed to suck her dry and he would possess a fortune.

In the meantime libels and indecent ballads and rhymes concerning her past were freely circulating. Even the King's name was openly ridiculed. The Duc de Choiseul, his sister the Duchesse de Grammont and their friends were spreading these ignoble refrains, Choiseul, sure of his strength and unquestionable authority, felt that he stood on a pedestal which nobody could reach. Jeanne was aware of all this malicious campaign, but by orders of Jean she ignored it. Seeing that this war of words was not effecting its purpose, the belligerent *grandes dames* decided to abstain from the Court ceremonies to show their animosity. His Majesty could no longer pretend not to notice the low sonnets and libels which were becoming more bawdy each day, and now added to the insults the abstention of many Court ladies letting it be known that they could not degrade themselves by being in the same building as the King's harlot. At Jeanne's card table others would walk away when timidly asked to join her game, men alleged that they had forgotten their money, so Jeanne, forlorn and alone, would leave her empty table.

Months passed and now Jeanne had almost ascended to the throne of France, but she confessed to Chon that she had lost her *joie de vivre*. Her laughs, her smiles, her every action had become artificial. The old days of Monsieur Labille the dressmaker, the Sundays at the Foire Saint-Germain, the collation under the trees and above all the excitement of a new lover, had gone, but, she would add, as all this had disappeared, she was intent to make 'my new way of life an historical event'.

The King suffered in his pride and love as he watched each evening during the different *divertissements* that Jeanne was more and more shunned by those who formed the social throng. She outshone them all in her loveliness, gowned in white made almost luminous by the precious stones which covered her gown, her fair hair falling in curls around her swan-like neck, caught up with diamond pins. She had invented this new way of dressing her hair; many of the ladies longed to imitate her, but they dared not for fear of being ostracized. So Jeanne was left to sit alone, or with her sole acquaintance, that gambler Madame de Bearn. Louis XV felt that this situation could not continue, he consulted the Duc de Richelieu and left it to him to break this intolerable position; he knew it was a formidable task. The person able to relax the unbearable tension would have to carry a great name and thus induce others to follow. The only one who might be enticed was the Maréchale de Mirepoix, ever on the alert for money, crippled with debts and spending what she did not have on useless stupidities. When they approached her on the subject it coincided with a time when she was being hard pressed by her creditors, she listened. She was requested to become head of the supposed Court of the King's mistress; besides this she should try to induce high-born ladies to join her. She asked for time to consider the proposition. A few days later the Maréchale, exhausted by the clamour of the menacing tradesmen, succumbed and declared herself ready to become the travelling and supper companion of the Comtesse Du

Barry, for a sum of a hundred thousand livres a year. Yet the old fairy Urgèle, as Society called her, was not sufficient; more ladies must surround the Comtesse. Perhaps the Duchesse de Valentinois might be considered, though she was scarcely conscious and quite mad, and on the point of death into the bargain; but her name would help to swell the forlorn few. She consented at once, not quite understanding why she was offered a sum of money. Another lady easily conquered by the golden livres was the Marquise de l'Hôpital, the mistress of the Prince de Soubise, whose reputation had nothing to lose. Then the great prize – the Princesse de Montmorency, who was urged to accept by her husband, who coveted the post of *menin* to the Dauphin, but all these dealings instead of reconciling the Court ladies, made them not only turn their heads away from Jeanne, but nearly spit at her and at the ladies who had lowered themselves for filthy lucre.[1]

Perhaps the most terrifying ordeal that Jeanne experienced in her present life was that first journey, when the King, bored beyond endurance by the attitude of his courtiers, decided on a sojourn at Choisy, one of his favourite domains, and for the first time she was directed to ride in the Monarch's coach alone with him. She was sitting conversing with Chon, when the message was delivered to her. For a few moments she seemed aghast, then in a voice of fury she exclaimed, 'No that I shall never do! I have suffered enough, shut within the walls of Versailles, but to proclaim my badge of disrepute to the citizens and peasants of France, while passing through their towns and villages, and worse to be jeered at by the rabble as the King's whore is beyond my courage. Surely Louis will not insist on such humiliation!'

But inexorably the time arrived when Jeanne was bade to enter the King's quilted coach, and to take her place by his side. All the protestations had been swept away, it was the etiquette and the rule must be obeyed. The endless cavalcade passed through the gates of Versailles on its way to Choisy. The sumptuous carriages contained Mesdames de France, the Dauphin, the remainder of the Royal Family, and following these, came the Court. The King

[1] Edmond et Jules de Goncourt – *La Du Barry*.

had punished a few of the ladies for their outrageous behaviour towards Madame Du Barry, by erasing their names from the list of guests. They were the Duchesse de Choiseul, the Duchesse de Grammont, the Comtesse de Brionne and the Comtesse d'Eglemont. Unfortunately this unfolded their anger still more, and their hatred became tenfold. As he looked through the small *vasistas* at the back of their coach, the King was jubilant, he smiled at Jeanne and said, 'We have won.' She was trembling as she saw the crowds watching the show, and replied, 'Perhaps we have won for the present, but what of the future?' A prophetic sentence!

It was during that time that Jeanne was able to show herself in a light different from that of merely radiating her beauty. She heard of a tragic case; a poor girl had given birth to a stillborn baby, and as she had not declared her pregnancy to the authorities, she was accused of infanticide, and condemned to the gallows. A young officer, Monsieur de Mandeville, who felt great pity for the girl's plight, decided to ask Madame Du Barry to intervene. He did not know her, but he had been told that she was kind, and he ventured a visit. When she knew all the details, she wrote at once a very touching letter to the Chancellor of France, and obtained the girl's pardon. This act of charity startled the nobility, who realized that after all she was not all superficial shine. Shortly after this, another tragedy took place. The Comte and Comtesse Louësme had been arrested and condemned to decapitation. Since they belonged to the nobility of France, the emotion this sentence created was enormous. The Comte and Comtesse who were crippled with debts to a fabulous extent, had been ordered by the Court of Justice to leave their château, which was to be sold to repay the creditors. When the bailiffs came to expel them from their ancestral home, the Comtesse in her anger shot one of the officers. Madame Du Barry determined to save them. She went to the King and knelt before him, declaring she would not raise herself until he had granted her request to save these unfortunate people. After some pleading, Louis, touched at his mistress's grief said, 'Madame I rejoice that the first act you implore me to do, should be an act of humanity.'

43

6

Louveciennes

One wonders if Jeanne ever really cared for Louis as a man. Even she, with her constant presence near him, never guessed his true nature. He seemed to carry about him the very essence of indolence, and of disinterest, his captivating eyes diffusing quiescence and at the same time a glint of dissipation. No one realized that behind that façade lived a man deeply interested in secret diplomatic affairs. To achieve his aims, he corresponded with his agents in Warsaw, St. Petersburg, Constantinople, London and Stockholm, through the Prince de Conti, leaving his Ministers to guess what was going on. Yet he achieved little since his constant fear was that these intrigues might be discovered by the Ministry. His most ambitious scheme was that the turbulent throne of Poland should be occupied by a French Prince.

During these months Choiseul was unconsciously weaving the net which looked unbreakable at the moment, but would prove in time unable to withhold his gigantic power which seemed unassailable. The revolting epigrams, the nauseating libels which were saturating the very air of Paris and the Provinces were becoming a danger, and were all aiming to smother Jeanne's name in filth. The King knew only too well from whence they emanated. On the other hand to acknowledge them would occasion an upheaval. He realized how indispensable Choiseul was for the country, how he could rely on him for governing, how tactfully Choiseul made it seem as if all was dictated by the King himself. Choiseul had rebuilt the Army and the Navy which had become almost non-existent after the seven year war. He had battled with the great feud concerning the Jesuits and had witnessed their dissolution. So, faced with this dilemma, Louis advised Jeanne to try to conciliate the Duc. In fact she liked him as a man, and would willingly have been a friend. She only wanted to live her life, unlike Madame de Pompadour she did not wish to mix in politics. She was simple minded and not ambitious and did not understand the intricacies of ruling. Choiseul on his side would also have liked to lead his life, absorbed in his power, but his wife the Duchesse de Choiseul, and his sister the Duchesse de Grammont would not let him rest. The King as a last resort advised Jeanne to ask the Minister to see her. His two women became frantic, they used all their energies to prevent this visit, but he paid no heed to them and went. Jeanne was charming, sincerely wishing his friendship, Choiseul was touched. As they sat facing each other it must have been a queer picture, Madame Du Barry surrounded by all the luxury blind love could create, beautiful, simple, no airs, just a very ordinary woman. A woman who had come from the lowest strata of society, who had led a life of prostitution. He, one of the exalted members of the *grande noblesse de France*, who now firmly held the reins of the country, leading it north, south, east and west as the whim took him, was now listening patiently to this wanton who was bargaining her friendship for his silence. Later when Louis XV entered that same room, Jeanne was alone flushed, excited; she ran up to him and exclaimed, 'All this cabal is over, he never avowed that he knew why I had asked him to come. No word was spoken on the subject near to our heart but we understood, and when leaving he said, "Madame La Comtesse you can trust me".' The Monarch smiled and replied, 'My dear child you do not know the "great" of this world, let us hope but let us beware.'

It was during the journey to Compiègne which followed the sojourn at Choisy that the Du Barry's triumph reached its zenith. The King offered her as a gift the small exquisite Château of Louveciennes, near Versailles. It was delightfully situated on a hill, from which she could gaze over the vastness of her lover's domains. 'The house is extremely pretty, but is small and lacks commodities,' wrote the Prince de Ligne. In reality it was the first important gift, with the exception of jewellery, that Louis had offered Jeanne. Up to now she had lived on the money Jean Du

Barry had loaned her, and Jean had been handsomely repaid by the Treasury. Jeanne Du Barry, the girl of the Paris streets owned one of the châteaux of France. In thanksgiving to the King she decided she would make it worthy to receive him. From this moment she changed from being modest in her expenditure to indulging in the greatest extravagance.

Louveciennes was becoming a miniature Versailles. The Goncourts tell us of the marble walls, the exquisitely decorated ceilings, the allegorical figures which depicted Louis XV and Madame Du Barry, the unique collection of furniture, each piece a work of art. The delightful aquarelle of Moreau le jeune, which the Louvre possesses, shows us the fête which Madame Du Barry offered the King on his first visit to her lovely domain. It takes us into her enchanting white and gold dining-room; a slight haze seems to envelop the whole room, caused by the innumerable crystal candelabras flashing with the sparks of hundreds of wax tapers. His Majesty presides at the head of the table, Jeanne decked in all her glory is beside him, they are encircled by the sumptuously clad guests. The men's *peruques*, and the ladies' powdered hair give the impression of a long white ribbon above all that gold and silver. The valets, lackeys, head butlers, the porters carrying the dishes, some in pale yellow liveries others in crimson ones. One can recognize Zamor, the small coloured boy, in pink velvet jacket and trousers, white turban, and carrying a small sword. He had been brought from Bengal, and given to Jeanne as a present; she cherished him tenderly, and spoiled him intensely. The crystal, the gold plate, the beautifully gowned women, the jewels, the men with their sashes, the crowd standing around allowed to look at the pageant, give us a picture of the time, which made the Court of France the criterion of supreme elegance.

Notwithstanding the lies and half truths which were flung around Versailles, and rebounding from its walls, defaming the name of a woman, that woman was beginning to intrigue Europe. Details of her past life were rife, her ascendance over the King's mind and senses was becoming limitless. Rumours of her secret but direct thrusts at Choiseul were being discussed abroad. Who

would survive the final battle, the Mistress or the Prime Minister?
This interested the different governments, after all it might influence policy and so alter the balance of power in the world. The
Comtesse Du Barry was now history. Horace Walpole arrived
from England on the 17th of September, 1769, and in a letter to
George Montagu, he describes how he rushed to Versailles to take
a look at the King of France's woman. He saw her in the chapel,
accompanied by her constant companion, her sister-in-law Chon.
They sat at the front of the altar, in the lower tribune. To his
surprise she wore no powder on her hair, or rouge on her cheeks.
She was attired in a simple *négligé* gown, and not in the *grande
toilette* which it had always been the rule to wear during religious
ceremonies. Walpole was shocked, he could not understand that
such decadence could be tolerated. The King must be ageing he
thought. The truth was that Louis, blinded by his passion, was
gradually losing all sense of decorum, and allowed Madame Du
Barry to resume some of the free and easy ways of her former life.
She was now so sure of her position that she developed more and
more a taste for a life of complete self-indulgence, and a distaste
for the etiquette of the *grande toilette*. She declared her hair was
too beautiful to be hidden by powder. Mme. Vigée-Lebrun tells us
that she refused to rouge her cheeks, which was the rule at Court.
Even at the suppers in the *petits cabinets*, which had always been
attended by ladies in grand habits, she introduced the *petites robes*
simple and voluptuous at the same time, scarcely concealing the
breasts. Louis took all this licentiousness naturally, it revived and
stimulated his diminishing senses. Walpole returned to England
amazed and shocked.

Although the Comtesse Du Barry's existence had the semblance
of immense prosperity, and seemed the apotheosis of all desires,
there was one dark cloud which overshadowed her felicity, and
tormented her unceasingly. What would her position be when
Marie Antoinette, the Austrian princess, arrived to marry the
Dauphin? She realized that she stood high, though only as an
impure figure, she might not survive in the presence of a pure,
innocent Imperial child. This fear intensified as the date of the

arrival drew near. When the dreaded moment was almost at hand, Jeanne debated within herself if it would be more tactful to leave Versailles during the marriage festivities or wait until she was asked to do so. In anticipation she had ordered sumptuous clothes, in case she was bidden to the ceremonies. In her dilemma she consulted the Duc de Richelieu, who told her to brave it out. He knew the King, who might suddenly see the light, and resolve to live without her, and not recall her if she was absent.

Today it was officially announced that H.I.H. the Archduchess Marie Antoinette, now Dauphine of France, was journeying towards her new country.

After endless negotiations and delays, the enchanting Dauphine Marie Antoinette was reaching the halting stations which had been assigned to her. She was fourteen years old. She sat in her coach bewildered and yet terribly lonely having to smile and acknowledge gracefully speeches which she did not comprehend. The language was so florid and intricate, much above her understanding, and the dread of all she had been told of the grandeur of the Court of France terrorized her. France was almost delirious with joy, for so long the population had been deprived of any respectable excitement. The huge cavalcade, three hundred and forty horses, which had to be changed at every post, was slowly reaching the French frontier. On arrival there, amid much ceremony the young girl had to be divested of all the clothes she wore, as nothing Austrian was allowed to her. She was quickly redressed in a chemise of French silk, petticoats from Paris, stockings from Lyons, shoes from the most celebrated shoemaker. A ring she had always worn was taken from her, and at the last moment even the baptismal cross she had worn since her birth was snatched away. She bade farewell to her household, and all those she had known for so long, who had ever been near her. She entered alone, that France, which would in time become the tragic stage for her martyrdom.

Louis XV, who had come to meet her with the Dauphin, descended from his chariot and went forward to greet her, next to him walked awkwardly the bridegroom. The young Archduchess forestalled them, jumped out of her berline and with a graceful reverence almost knelt before the King, who raised her at once, and embraced her tenderly. Then he introduced her to the Dauphin who, resenting the whole performance, kissed her cheek. The crowd was overcome, and many wept with emotion. The Dauphine was brought to Mesdames de France and the remainder of the Royal Family. Prettily she expressed the honour she felt and hoped she might be worthy of belonging to France. The Duc de Richelieu looked for Jeanne Du Barry, she was not there! The Monarch was so overjoyed at the sight of the enchanting child that evidently he had overlooked Jeanne's absence.

That night at the banquet the Comtesse Du Barry was present, outshining all. The King had regained his consciousness!

The Duc de Lauzun in his memoirs describes the scenes which took place for the marriage of the Dauphin and Dauphine. 'I assisted at them all,' he tells us. 'The wealth and magnificence of the men's habits was beyond imagination. They were laden with gold and precious stones, so that they could scarcely sustain their weight. The King's habit weighed forty pounds. I being of slight build nearly succumbed under the weight of mine. On the 16th of May, the day of the marriage, the greatest religious ceremonies took place. The religious display bordered on the unreal, all the lavish rites of the Catholic faith were enacted. The Dauphine, so young, promising to carry through life the duties, the meaning of which she knew nothing. After the regal marriage, the Royal State banquet took place in public; anyone could attend and stare at the Royal Family. Later in the Grand apartments the King established himself at a card table in the famous Galerie des Heures. All who had been presented had the honour of passing before His Majesty. A little way away from his table sat ladies at smaller ones playing games of cards, others looked on sitting on folding stools. At the hour of eleven there was a stir, the Duc de Richelieu advanced into the immense gallery and in a high pitched voice announced that the reception was over and the courtiers were dismissed, then bowing low to the Dauphin and Dauphine told them the hour for their *coucher* was at hand. Here now the etiquette became rigorous. A procession headed by the Duc de Richelieu, followed by the King and Royal Family reached the nuptial bedroom. The large ornamental bed whose columns supporting the canopy were surmounted by clusters of waving plumes, the blankets and sheets were drawn back ready to receive the newly wed. The Dauphine was shown into a sumptuous dressing-room to undress, and the Dauphin was taken straight into an adjacent apartment. He was helped by several valets to have all his clothes taken off. Then his head valet handed the Dauphin's nightshirt to the Duc d'Orléans, who in turn with a bow handed it to the King. His Majesty with a few kind words slipped it over the head of his grandson.

'A similar ceremony took place for the Dauphine. She was undressed by her ladies, her nightgown was handed to the Duchesse de Chartres who passed it over the Dauphine's head. The young princess was led to the great bedroom and put to bed. When the Dauphine was ready, a procession formed outside the room. There was a knock on the door and the King followed by all the Royal Family and the official members of the Court brought in the Dauphin and aided him into the bed. The curtains were drawn, but were immediately drawn back again, and once more the Royal Family and all those who had the *entrée* filed past the young shy prince and princess, made a low bow and left the room.'

After the official marriage ceremonies the rejoicings went on for several days, banquets, theatricals, galas, fireworks, balls, fairy scenes on the lake. Marie Antoinette was so overcome, and exhausted by all this display, she scarcely had time to analyse her days, but one woman in the throng intrigued her, a woman who stood above all others in her beauty, and who was never far from the person of the King. At last she asked one of her brothers-in-law, the Comte de Provence, who she was. He answered, 'Her role is to amuse Grandpapa.' She knew little of life and took it naturally. A few days later her other brother-in-law, the Comte d'Artois, less discreet explained in detail the true position of Jeanne. The crude truth shattered the young girl, instinctive revulsion took root, for that woman whose wages were earned by infamy, and who flaunted her uncleanliness before the world. Marie Antoinette could find no word strong enough to express her disgust – as she knew none. Her mother, the Empress Marie-Therese had never tolerated any scandal or even the slightest allusion to the ordinary facts of life to be mentioned in her presence.

That evening the Dauphine glanced at this woman as if she had looked at an evil spirit. The festivities were now virtually at an end and the Dauphine would have to take up her position as the first lady of the land. That evening she was to receive the Court ladies, as they would pass one by one before her. The etiquette was thus – the Dauphine was to say an amiable word of greeting to each of them. No one could speak until she had broken the silence. In an old book of the times (of which I have unfortunately forgotten the name or author) a description is given of this scene. 'The brilliantly-lit Hall was dazzling, the Dauphine stood before a large gilt *fauteuil*, almost a throne, she was surrounded by her newly named Court. Her *grande maitresse* the Comtesse de Noailles, stood near her. The young Dauphine seemed the very symbol of grandeur, of dignity and yet one guessed that beneath it all lay bubbling youth. As the ladies made a deep reverence she smiled and said, "I am pleased to make your acquaintance." The long queue wound its way through the vast rooms, a stir went through the courtiers standing by, they seemed to spring to attention, the Comtesse Du Barry was making her reverence. As she rose and stood for barely a second before the future Queen of France, waiting for her few words of welcome, Marie Antoinette turned her head away and spoke to one of her gentlemen standing by. Jeanne Du Barry swayed slightly and went on, as the next lady followed, the Dauphine resumed her words of graciousness.'

✢   ✢   ✢

Louis XV King of France whom all the world envied was alone in his private cabinet pondering, he knew that he was being despised, and that his liaison with Jeanne, and her reputation were being discussed in all the important capitals of Europe. It was recorded that he was lowering the magnificence and glory of his country which he had sworn to uphold. Yet he felt powerless to alter the cause of his distress. Above all, to add to the tragedy of his plight, Monsieur de Beaumont, Archbishop of Paris, had asked to be received and with great kindness and touching solicitude had unfolded the object of his visit. Madame Louise, the King's youngest daughter, had asked him to inform her father that she wished to enter the Order of Carmelites. The shock had been terrible. Now he was alone, the Archbishop had left. Suddenly he was startled out of his tragic broodings by a gentle knock on the door, and his daughter Madame Louise entered the room; she knelt at his feet and in a few words she told him she had come in person to ask his permission to enter the Carmelite order. Very touchingly she continued, that for a long time she had desired this, but her love for him had held her back. The world meant nothing to her now, above all the immorality and sins against Almighty God were killing her. She would try and make atonement in a small way for those who had forgotten their Creator. The only favour she begged of her father was not to mention her decision until the doors of the cloister had closed on her for ever. The King experienced a moment of defeat, he realized that his child was sacrificing her future for his redemption, but still those inescapable poisonous fangs went deeper than parental love, and he let her go. Of all his daughters Madame Louise was the most frivolous and gay, she loved luxury and had even been known to yield to mild flirtation. It was said that when the Monarch came to Madame Adelaide's room the morning after Louise's departure, and with tears running down his face announced to her that her sister had gone away that night, Madame Adelaide in a choked voice cried, 'With whom?'

7

The Fall of Choiseul

All the golden clouds enveloping the Court of France could not conceal that in truth the whole of the Kingdom was steeped to its very core in misery. Constantly the rabble would muster around the Prince's coaches, crying out, 'Bread, we want bread!' The coachmen would whip up the horses and unconcernedly gallop through the crowd, scattering them, not hesitating to send them rolling in the road. The mortality among new-born babies was horrifying, so many died only a few hours or days after their birth, people scarcely noticed that a baby had been born, they were buried like carrion with no pretence of formality. The hospitals, the Military Hospital, the Hôpital de la Charité, and the Hôtel Dieu, did not suffice to care for all the sick, the maimed, and the injured. Monsieur Necker tells us that when visiting one of these places he saw six old men in one bed. The prisons were nests of infections, overflowing with humanity, as people were arrested on the slightest suspicion, thrown into these cesspools and forgotten. The streets were puddles of filth, drains were non-existent, all natural functions took place anywhere without any pretence of bashfulness. All these appalling conditions were known, but they were considered inevitable, evils which nothing could alter. The hovels in which the populace existed were black holes, their food consisted of what they could scavenge from the markets after the farmers had ceased selling. The whole of France stank of want, and yet people accepted it knowing no better and no way out. Of course there were charitable people, and there was much talk of helping the needy, but in reality little was done. Yet Louveciennes was becoming a paradise of beauty.

The governments of Europe were justified in their disquiet concerning the feud between the Du Barry and the mighty Duc de Choiseul, hourly it was intensifying and becoming almost a national issue. All realized the growing influence of the King's mistress, but still the Duc was a strong opponent. Yet unbeknown to all were three formidable adversaries at work, determined to destroy Choiseul: they were the Duc d'Aiguillon, Monsieur Maupeou, and lastly the Abbé Terray.

After a long absence the Duc d'Aiguillon had returned to the capital. His tenure of office as Governor of Brittany had not been a happy one. This dour, stolid and steel minded race had resented his affected manner from the start. Yet d'Aiguillon was a courtier of the finest mettle, and able to steer his course to his own satisfaction. He was ambitious. Although a follower of the Richelieu faction he decided to bide his time and find out for himself the extent of Louis XV's infatuation with Madame Du Barry. After all Choiseul was a man of great ability and farsightedness, and his abhorrence for the King's mistress might be well founded. D'Aiguillon had not long to wait. One evening when he was standing in a small circle not far from the Monarch, the King was talking to his mistress; while doing so he dropped his snuffbox. She bent down immediately, and kneeling on one knee held the box up to him, the King raised her and murmured in his caressing voice, but loud enough to be heard by all, 'Madame it is for me to take this position and for always.' D'Aiguillon knew that the vessel to alight on was the one on whose poop stood the figurehead of Madame Du Barry.

Monsieur Maupeou the Chancellor was so far a creature of Choiseul. The Minister did not entirely trust him but he had secured this high post for him on account of his subtle intelligence. Maupeou was slyly veering his course towards Madame Du Barry. He was a dreaded figure at Court, his exterior was as unprepossessing as the dark alleys of his tortuous soul. His mere presence was enough to petrify the courtier who had only dared dream of crossing swords with him. Many had been astounded when Choiseul led such an unscrupulous blackguard into the Ministry. The Duc had tersely replied, 'I know the man is not to be trusted as a friend, but he is the most capable in France for this post just now. If he makes himself troublesome, I shall deal with him accordingly.' The first clash between Choiseul and Maupeou came over the appointment of the Abbé Terray to the Ministry of Finance. The blow to Choiseul's prestige had been all the more severe since he himself had proposed a candidate for this most critical post. The Abbé was now Comptroller General of France. The looks, ways and means of the protégé matched perfectly those of his sponsor. Yet those two feared personages were now concerting their efforts to save the shaky Treasury. To achieve their ends they decided to abolish the antiquated system by which the propertied classes could manage to escape the payment of most taxes. The Parliaments who stood for these propertied classes, as they themselves were part of them, were up in arms against these measures and determined to resist them at all costs. Maupeou had realized that France had approached a crossroad, either the King or the Parliaments must give way. He had resolved to crush the latter and restore once again the central authority to the Monarch. In his clear icy mind he saw that the mistress would be the ideal medium through whom he could attain his ends. He would flatter her, side with her against her enemies at Court, and above all gracefully allow her whims and extravagances to be met by the Treasury. Having gained her favour, she would be an easy prey, who would persuade the King of the soundness of the Chancellor's schemes, and cajole the Monarch into granting the laws and reforms he had devised.

Jeanne's repugnance to be drawn into politics kept her away from any political question. It bored her; she really did not care one way or another what happened! But like a swarm of bees the different politicians pursued her, not showing their game openly, but each of them determined to benefit. The only time the Duc d'Aiguillon had seen her as yet was on the night of the snuffbox incident. He spoke to his uncle the Duc de Richelieu of his wish to know her more intimately: so it was arranged that the handsome nephew should be invited to one of the *soupers* of the *petits cabinets*. The night Jeanne received him her beauty seemed to belong to the immortal, all in white, in one of the simple *toilettes* she had introduced, amiable, gay, witty, she captivated the young Duc. Nor was she indifferent to his manly attraction. He was young and *svelte*, his skin had the glow of health, and as he bent towards her when addressing her, a certain sensual charm emanated from his person. Ah! the old life stood in front of her. If she were but free! Closing her eyes she murmured a few words to the King who tenderly raised her hand to his lips, she must be careful, all the guests were watching. The flesh is weaker than the spirit, friendship or perhaps a stronger bond sprang up between the Comtesse Du Barry and the Duc d'Aiguillon, but the future will show!

The Duc de Chaulnes had just died, thus leaving free the post of Commander of the King's Guard. Choiseul had already a candidate for this very important position. The Commander had the entry to His Majesty's presence at any time to report on the daily events, and advise the King. Without consulting him the King chose d'Aiguillon, Choiseul's fury rose to a tempest, he knew it was the work of the Du Barry. In his discomposure he acted like a lunatic, and spared no one, in effigy he had the mistress dragged in the dung of the alleys of Paris, and went even so far as to blame the King openly. All this was reported to His Majesty at the daily interviews of the new Commander.

Louis was aware that Choiseul's jealousy and morbid hatred of Jeanne was usurping his reason, but he also knew how ably the Prime Minister had led the country, how sound his views had ever been. No! he could not reign without him, who was there to equal his skill? D'Aiguillon guessed that Choiseul was aware of the intrigues hatched against him, and that he was implacably determined to risk all, to retain his power.

France was in a turmoil of unrest, the Parliaments were claiming their reforms against the King's wishes. Maupeou and Terray were undermining Choiseul's government, d'Aiguillon's old enemies, the Bretons, were bringing a lawsuit against him, questioning his honesty during his governorship; this could be disastrous for him. In tears Jeanne Du Barry begged the King to quash the whole case, this meant the King should hold a *Lit de Justice*, in which he would declare that any further allusion to the lawsuit of the Duc d'Aiguillon, should end. All the books and evidence which the Bretons had brought forth in accusation must be destroyed. The *Lit de Justice* was held, with untold solemnity, and the tears of the mistress of the King were dried by the decree, and the handsome Commander was acquitted without even making an appearance. The indignation of the Parliaments was terrific, Choiseul had excused himself from attending when the King held this *Lit de Justice*, but the result gave him the certainty that the concubine's role was nearing despotism!

One evening, the Duc de Choiseul was alone in his study, it was late, yet he did not notice the hour, sleep had evaded him since some time. He was trying to write a letter to the King, a letter of apologies, and resolutions to make amends, he could not word it, it sounded futile at this time of crisis. The infamous woman would hold it up in triumph, and the odious cringing hounds at her feet would yelp with glee. No! only a greater stirring event could save him. A WAR! Yes, a war. It would sweep aside all these vermin! Louis XV would once again cling to him. Yes! Yes! a war, but where?

That day the Ministry had received news that there was an annoying dispute going on in a remote part off the coast of the Argentine, the Falkland Islands, where for many years English families had settled, and raised cattle, never doubting anybody might disturb their security. Suddenly the Spanish remembered that it was territory which belonged to them, and retook possession. The British were outraged at this and decided to send an ultimatum to Spain. England was strong, and Spain weak, but King Ferdinand VI relied on the *Pacte de Famille* which had been instituted by Louis XIV; it consisted in a pact of mutual assistance between the Bourbon rulers in case of war. Choiseul of his own accord sent encouraging messages to the King of Spain, and at the same time veiled threats to England. Louis XV who was not interested in the Falklands, and dreaded war, told Choiseul to inform Spain tactfully that France was not ready for an armed conflict, the Parliaments were too unsettled and the whole country far from tranquil. Choiseul paid no heed to the warning, and continued his tactics; it looked as if he had lost his balance. The Duc d'Aiguillon was badgering the Du Barry, unearthing every scrap of detrimental evidence, and vastly exaggerating the half truths against Choiseul. The King was desperately trying to keep his reason between the different factions, fearing the fury of the people if Choiseul was dismissed and the loathed Ministers left to govern. Above all he dreaded that the blame would fall on Jeanne as being the concoctor of the whole plot.

Like so many Emperors and Monarchs have done before and after him, the King would not allow those around him to offer their advice, to take heed of them would be giving away some of his prerogatives, thus Louis XV was undergoing a moment of great indecision. Choiseul's enemies resolved to hasten his fall, otherwise he might regain all that he had lost, and it would mean their own destruction. On the 21st of December 1770 Madame Du Barry duly instructed by d'Aiguillon, once more broached the subject of Choiseul's perfidy. Louis exasperated by this perpetual nagging, said, 'I shall do nothing unless I have direct proofs, the Duc de Choiseul has always been a loyal servant and I will not allow his name to be smeared, unless I am convinced of the truth of the accusations.' Jeanne asked him to send for d'Aiguillon, who came at the King's command. The King, flushed and angry, repeated what he had just said to Jeanne. The Commander hesitated for a few minutes and said, 'Sire, you do not believe us, but there is an easy way to discover the truth; ask the Abbé de la Ville, he is one of the Duc de Choiseul's clerks, and a man of high repute, perhaps your Majesty could ask his advice.' So that night in the greatest secrecy the Abbé was ushered into the King's presence. The King asked him how far the negotiations concerning the conflict between Spain and England had proceeded. The Abbé said that he did not know – although working in the Duc's private office he never saw the dispatches, as the Prime Minister never allowed anyone but himself to take note of them, but if His

Majesty desired to know the exact position, he advised him to command the Prime Minister to inform the King of Spain that on no account would he be drawn into a war, since he desired peace. If Monsieur de Choiseul made any objection it would prove that he was for war. The King seemed very nervous. The Goncourts tell us that when agitated his chin would tremble. So much depended on the result of this question concerning his Minister. The next morning when he entered the room where the Ministers were assembled, without preliminary ceremony the King ordered Choiseul to send a letter to Grimaldi the Spanish Prime Minister and inform him definitely that on no account would he take part in a conflict. For a few moments Choiseul was disconcerted, he had just sent a dispatch to Spain proposing a new plan: answering His Majesty, he said that before sending this letter it would be better to wait for the reply of Grimaldi to his latest dispatch. If his proposals were not acceptable there would always be time to forward the letter as His Majesty suggested. The King rose, the tremor of his chin seemed to accentuate, and without pronouncing a word he stalked angrily to the door, in his rage almost wrenching the handle, and without waiting for the usual ceremony of being escorted out, slammed it behind him. The Ministers looked at one another, some of them had not had time to rise from their seats. Choiseul alone seemed outwardly unconcerned, but doubtless flinched inwardly. Maupeou and the Abbé Terray exchanged glances, which they understood, and the Monarch could doubt no longer!

In those marvellous halls of Versailles that evening amid the pomp and ceremonies, wit, laughter and amorous whispers, two people were subjected to deep mental stress. One was the King, undecided, dreading the issue which must come, the exile of his right-hand man. The other, the victim to be, who realized nothing could absolve him now that he was being submerged by the venomousness of the woman he hated and of her gang of vultures. Yet their distress was apparent to no one, His Majesty talked graciously and smiled at the courtiers' witty remarks, the Duc de Choiseul strolled, greeting with an amusing word his friends and foes, and not showing an inkling of the ache of his heart, in reality two brave men.

Before his private *coucher* Louis XV sent for Monsieur de la Vrillière and bade him to take a *lettre de cachet* to the Duc de Choiseul in the early morning. It was late, past midnight, the King had chosen that hour so as to be alone and that no one should witness his grief. The fateful billet had gone. He dismissed his valets, and in a few moments he would lie next to the woman for whom he had sacrificed so much. Had he been right? Now fate had swept him rapidly along and shown him the way, yes, it was showing the way to an end. He felt tired, would God forgive his unruly life? As usual he knelt on his gilded prie-dieu and recited his nightly prayers, he had always done so ever since a child, then taking up a flambeau, slowly climbed the small staircase and entered the Comtesse Du Barry's room.

The next morning, on the 24th of December 1770, Choiseul was handed by Monsieur de La Vrillière the order of exile. The order exiled him to his country château, Chanteloup. He was allowed twenty-four hours to prepare his departure from Paris. The Duc and Duchesse de Choiseul bowed down with calm and great dignity to the brutal command, without resentment they prepared to leave their Paris home. The Duc did not seek to see the King. When the public learned of the dismissal, they perceived only one reason, that the Minister was being sacrificed and the country placed in peril for the sake of appeasing the hatred of the infamous whore.

Scarcely had the news spread than the capital seemed to vibrate in a state of alarm. The streets were crowded, all were anxious to hear if this could really be true. The people questioned each other, utter strangers spoke to utter strangers, deploring the catastrophe. Around the ducal house the mob was so great that none of the Duc's friends could penetrate to it. At last a few intimates, at their head the Duc de Chartres, forced their way in, to embrace him for the last time. Twenty-four hours later the Duc and Duchesse de Choiseul left their home. The disgrace became a triumph, on both sides of the road from his residence, rue de Richelieu to the Barrière de l'Enfer, every point of vantage was occupied. People climbed on roofs, on windows and on trees, all intent on showing their sympathy. When the exiles appeared in their carriage cheering and blessing broke forth, and the enthusiasm became unrestrained. The squad of gendarmes who had been stationed near the house to see that the King's orders should be carried out, were rapidly dispersed. It seemed as if the whole of Paris had assembled to show their affection.

The horde of fanatics who followed the ducal coach, which had to be driven slowly, was almost hysterical, and accompanied it well beyond the city. Choiseul tried to answer the crowd by smiling and giving the impression of great calm, but once he and the Duchesse had crossed the barrier of Paris he wept. That same moment at Versailles, Louis was still wondering. A heavy weight oppressed him, his sleep had been troubled, Jeanne's allure had not reached him. Lately his response to her wonderful seduction had decreased, she was still the only woman he loved, but perhaps he was ageing, and desire weakening. She herself had realized the truth and had even suggested that only now and then should he share her couch. Perhaps he should accept her cautionary advice, and yet that would be admitting his failing strength. His musings were disturbed, the Duc d'Aiguillon asked to be received. Half smiling, half trying to ridicule the story, in the fewest words he casually spoke of the scene which was disturbing Paris. Louis was swift to interpret the truth and danger. He sent immediately for Richelieu and bade him to inform him detail by detail of what had taken place, and the state of things at the moment. D'Aiguillon had been dismissed from the room. Richelieu described the events having just arrived from the capital. In a voice of anger the King shouted, 'My subjects will never forgive me, and perhaps they are right!'

The King in his *lettre de cachet* had stipulated that Choiseul could receive only his immediate family, and anyone else desiring to visit him had to obtain his permission. This order was never observed, it would have been impossible to do so, as from the very next day of their exile almost the whole of Paris drove to visit the Ducal couple. As an exile in his princely abode, the Duc de Choiseul was a greater celebrity than during his Ministry.

As the days passed, rumours of life at Chanteloup travelled to the capital. The grandeur, the luxury of the establishment surpassed that of Versailles, guests came and went in a continuous *va-et-vient*. The King's curiosity was constantly aroused by reports of the magnificence of the Duc and Duchesse de Choiseul's life at Chanteloup. We must turn to the Duc de Lauzun, his nephew, who describes for us in the minutest detail the fairy-like existence of the château.

'The life at Chanteloup is enchanting,' wrote the Duc de Lauzun, 'the greatest liberty is accorded to each one. Life becomes so easy as all live it as they choose. Every possible attraction is available, waiting to be tasted. Hunting, riding, boating, libraries filled with books, carriages waiting to take lovers to some retreat, in fact Chanteloup is a paradise of pleasure. At eight o'clock a transformation scene takes place, the Court etiquette becomes *de rigueur*. The guests gather in the drawing-room, men wear court dress or uniform with decorations, the ladies are in *grand paniers*, superbly adorned with gold and silver flowers, with pearls and diamonds, and displaying that exquisite grace with which their long sojourn at Versailles had endowed them. It is the exact replica of what takes place at the Court of Louis XV, but it seems a thousand times more beautiful. While waiting for the hour of supper, people play games such as tric trac, or take part in the witty and scintillating conversations. At nine o'clock the large doors of the dining hall are thrown open and the banquet announced. The host and hostess take in the principal guests, and with ceremony the others follow according to their rank. The food is good and sustaining, but simple. On leaving the dining hall each one reads his letters, it is the time for the post to arrive, it creates the occasion for much gossip, many confidences are exchanged, only to be whispered openly next day. Then the card games start, and later still one of the two orchestras play – dancing for the young ones, reminiscing for the older ones. On retiring to bed each person is accompanied by a lackey holding a candelabra, and wrapped in the comfort of the four-poster beds one sleeps and dreams in peace.'

8

Triumph – the move to Versailles

War was imminent between Spain and England, the Duc de Choiseul had been deposed, the country was wrought up, Europe on the *qui vive*. Yet a child of fifteen, the Dauphine, remained in her proud attitude. She continued to look above the Du Barry's head, whenever she perceived her. Mesdames de France's influence was abetting her in her determination to ignore that unashamed woman. Lately the disdain of Marie Antoinette had taken extreme measures. When obliged to pass near her she would sneer loudly and make a movement of drawing herself away as if afraid she might touch her. Jeanne, who grieved at the insults, complained to the King, he himself could not avoid noticing these degrading remarks and obvious manifestations. He had been informed by Choiseul before his exile that through the Comte Mercy d'Argenteau, the Austrian Envoy, the Empress Marie-Therese had urged her daughter Marie Antoinette to alter her manner towards the Comtesse Du Barry. Choiseul had added that it was difficult for such a strait-laced woman to insist that her child should befriend a mistress of the King. Louis XV had been furious with the Minister for such utterance but had to acknowledge it was justified. Now it was going too far, and he would send for the Envoy and make him remonstrate with the Dauphine and point out that her behaviour was unwise as she was annihilating his affection for her. The offence was not only her manner towards the person whose friendship he valued, but above all the defiance and criticism she allowed herself to show towards him as grandfather and Monarch. As the King stormed away in his displeasure the Count stood bewildered:

'But, Sire, I dare not reprimand the Dauphine, I am only the servant of her mother the Empress.'

The King, in all authority said, 'If you do not, I shall find means of forcing her!'

The Count with a low bow withdrew, and turning to Richelieu who had witnessed the scene, murmured, 'All this display for Jeanne Vaubernier, against an Austrian Archduchess.'

With pressure from all sides Marie Antoinette gave way, but she affirmed that only one short phrase would she utter to Madame Du Barry. So it was settled, the different parties informed, that on the next evening after the theatre the Count Mercy would stand by Madame Du Barry and engage her in a short conversation. At this moment the Dauphine would casually approach them, speak to the Envoy and at the same time address the Comtesse. Slowly that evening the Dauphine was making her way towards Madame Du Barry and the Count. The plan was working to time, when Madame Adelaide, one of the favourite's strongest opponents, hastened forward guessing the plot, and taking Marie Antoinette's arm said, 'It is late, we must retire.' The Dauphine not knowing what to do next followed her aunt. In reality the scene must have been rather ludicrous, the King looking intently, the Count feeling frustrated, Madame Du Barry almost in tears, and the Court smiling.

The Count Mercy who had worked himself to a state of near prostration the night before and had nearly collapsed when the eagerly awaited scheme had failed, in addition received a severe dispatch that morning from the Empress, reprimanding him for his want of zeal in not influencing the Dauphine politically and not exposing to her that her behaviour might damage the good relationship of France with Austria if she continued to antagonize the Monarch. Louis XV was devoted to her, and friendly with her country, but he was human and if too outraged an excuse could easily be found to break that friendship. Mercy flew to Versailles and asked for an immediate audience with the Dauphine. Marie Antoinette read the letter, a sullen look came into her eyes – how lovely she is, thought Mercy. He waited for an outburst of rebellion; instead an appearance of utter dejection came into those eyes, and slowly she answered:

'I have striven against most of the people here to keep my soul pure, away from acknowledging the filth which encloses my grandfather, but I have been condemned by all those who should have supported me, even my own mother insists that I should bend my head to a shameless sinner.'

The Envoy begged her to submit. The whole plan of the previous evening would be repeated that night. The Dauphine would accomplish her act and not heed any interruption, as the Envoy was bending low over that childlike hand Marie Antoinette said, 'Remember, only one phrase.'

That night the Court seemed particularly brilliant. His Majesty after the usual banquet prior to the games of cards, watched once more the favourite in all her beauty, waiting slightly apprehensive for what would follow, scarcely answering Mercy's conversation, who was equally anxious. From afar Mercy perceived the lovely young figure approaching, by then he could no longer concentrate on the subject on which he was speaking, he looked at his companion, she was unconsciously breaking her fan to bits. The Dauphine stood by Mercy, said a few words, and turning to Jeanne Du Barry, without looking at her said, 'There are many people at Versailles this evening.' At last the agony of so many months was lifted, the Dauphine may never address her again, but the ignominy of being an absolute outcast was over, eight words had perhaps saved Europe.

Jeanne Du Barry's greatest impediments were lifted, Choiseul was gone and the Dauphine had broken that terrible silence. In her freedom from direct worry she allowed herself the liberty of power. Chon still lived with her, but now scarcely counted in Jeanne's life, Jean Du Barry had entirely disappeared. Jeanne lost all sense of values, the jewellers, modistes, artists, inventors were displaying their fascinating wares each morning, she did not even inquire the worth of the priceless pieces she purchased. Louveciennes was engulfing millions, and so was the existence she led. Terray paid out discreetly, but after all it was but a pinprick compared to the exorbitant sums that were wasted on the management of the country. Then one day a mysterious message reached her, saying, 'Beware of the future, reflect, stop while there is still time. Revenge will be severe.' Laughingly she showed it to the Duc de Richelieu, who taking it in his hand let it flutter into the blazing fire.

In reality it was then, wrote Talleyrand, that Madame Du Barry commenced to play the rôle of *grande favorite*. Liberated from her greatest foe, she moved into that enchanting apartment at Versailles. The vastness of the rooms at Versailles endangered all privacy. It was with the arrival of Queen Marie Leczinska that the *mansardes* were transformed into those elegant apartments, sleeping chambers, boudoirs, salons, galleries, among them the famous *petits cabinets*, where the King's private supper-parties took place. When Madame Du Barry became possessor of that part of the château, she demanded its entire re-embellishment. What had sufficed for Marie Leczinska was not worthy of the Comtesse Du Barry. So the command went forth. Instantly the greatest artists of the period set to work. In a few weeks the metamorphosis was accomplished and the Comtesse deigned to occupy the 'whim' which had cost millions of livres. The wondrous beauty was a revelation, the heavy gilding of the past, the *Vernis Martin* had vanished, it was the innovation of the Louis XV era in all its flamboyant ornate style. Jeanne's bedroom was over the King's, a small staircase united the rooms. Madame Du Barry's sleeping apartment was an unbelievable dream. The couch appeared to consist of precious metal, the wood entirely covered by the finest gilding. Slender columns rose to the canopy, from which delicately chiselled bunches of laurels, roses and myrtle hung in profusion, in the midst two beautifully sculptured doves amorously cooed. A cover of exquisite white, shimmering brocade embroidered with bouquets of roses reposed on the couch and dropped on to the first step of the dais, and a carpet of silver lampas covered the dais on which the bedstead stood. Cupboards, dressing-table, writing-desk in satin wood, were inlaid with reproductions of Watteau paintings in priceless china. Curtains, chairs, all were covered with the same shimmering brocade as the couch. One large armchair stood near the bed, it was for the King, no one else was allowed to sit in it.

As a rule each morning at eight o'clock, the King's first valet would knock at Jeanne Du Barry's bedroom, and announce the time. His Majesty would then noiselessly descend by the private staircase and gain his own couch. The valet would rumple the sheets, dent the pillows to disguise the fact that His Majesty had only just stepped into his stately bed. So the *grand lever* started. Meanwhile the Comtesse Du Barry slept on until nine o'clock, then her head dresser followed by a bevy of attendants would glide back the golden shutters, and 'Venus' would open her eyes amid lace sheets and cushions of the finest gossamer tissues. Several of her attendants would lead her to a heavily perfumed bath. While she floated in this scented water her letters would be read, never anything very interesting, mostly demands for money or protection. On returning to her room she would be dressed in a number of petticoats trimmed with exquisite lace and a filmy *déshabillé*. Zamor would offer her on a gold tray a cup of coffee. Later at her dressing-table the famous coiffeurs would be announced, Monsieur Nokelle for the important occasions, and Monsieur Berline for everyday events. When the coiffeurs had finished their delicate task of just allowing a minimum of powder to fall like a mist over her beautiful hair, she would dismiss them, and just dust her face with a thin cloud of powder, after which she would remove it with a small silver knife. She disliked using rouge, but it was etiquette, so with the tip of her finger she spread the dark toned red of the Court on her lovely skin. In the meantime the antechambers, the halls, the staircase would be filling up with different merchants waiting in hopes the Comtesse would be tempted by their treasures – which she generally was. So for nearly two hours jewellers, famous dressmakers, shoemakers, furniture dealers would parade, no price was asked, none given. When the different merchants left the *petits appartements* they all congratulated each other – they had just time to return to Paris, replenish their bags and boxes and recommence the same scene the next day. When the stampede had subsided His Majesty would pay a morning visit to his mistress. The courtiers who were also waiting to pay their respects to the 'deity', would withdraw until the King had left her bedroom, then rush like a whirlwind to kiss her hand. Much later she would take a drive. Other times she would be carried in her sedan chair around the park, Zamor, the little Indian boy whom she loved, was usually beside her. Nothing was too good for this child, she really worshipped him and had fantastic clothes made for him, in which he revelled. Often she would return early from her afternoon promenade, as the King lamented her absence. For the third or fourth time she would change her dress, tea would be served, no one was allowed to be present, just the King and herself. When the King repaired to the Council, Madame la Comtesse would give her audiences. Then came the most important time of the day, the *grande toilette* for the evening. After the supper the King usually held his card game in Jeanne's apartment. In another drawing-room a concert would take place. Her establishment had become very important, her staff was enormous, her whole way of living was amounting to a fairy tale, her liveries outshone by their magnificence those of the monarch.

Often the King's mistresses have been blamed for their reckless mode of living, but often unjustly. When one reflects that to satisfy these women's ambitions, poets, authors, painters, architects, have excelled in their skill, works of art and treasures untold have come into existence. Such were the *petits appartements* at Versailles, and the Château de Louveciennes, created by order of one woman. The latter became an enchanted 'Eden' for her harmonious beauty. In her research for perfection every item of her surroundings had to attain the ideal, so the caprice of the Comtesse Du Barry was the means by which France was enriched by many masterpieces.

The Comtesse Du Barry who had not known what the word politics meant now listened with interest to the politicians during her evening audiences, and with assurance bestowed her opinions and decisions as if she was the reigning Sovereign.

Madame du Deffand writes to Walpole, 'The Cabinet is not named yet, but what is certain is that the mistress only wants "her" creatures in it. It is said that the Duc d'Aiguillon will be Foreign Minister; considering their relations, it may be true. Louis with his usual indecision refused to be hurried.' It was during the festivities for the marriage of the Comte de Provence, later Louis XVIII, that the formation of a new Cabinet became acute. Louis was still vacillating, so Jeanne Du Barry decided to act. It was the 5th of June 1771. Monsieur de Chamfort tells the story:

'The Comtesse Du Barry summoned the Duc d'Aiguillon and informed him that this situation must terminate. "Tomorrow you will ask for an audience of the King, and you will thank him for having nominated you Minister of Foreign Affairs!" Then she went to the King, and said, "Tomorrow the Duc d'Aiguillon will thank you for having named him Minister of Foreign Affairs." The King did not answer. Next day, d'Aiguillon, frightened, refused to go, but the *grande favorite* ordered him to do so, he obeyed her and presented himself before the Monarch, bowing deeply, he waited for His Majesty to speak, but the King remained silent. d'Aiguillon, remembering the Du Barry's injunction not to hesitate but to thank him for having bestowed on him the title of Minister of Foreign Affairs, again obeyed her, and spoke up in a tremulous voice, Louis XV did not utter a syllable. Bowing d'Aiguillon retired and immediately took up his new duties.'

The scene was reported to the Choiseul party, which meant nearly the whole of Society, and their fury was unrestrained. The news spread quickly beyond Versailles; the resentment against the hated Ministers grew, but above all of them stood the King's mistress, to the people she was becoming the symbol of vice. They feared her! She had bewitched their Monarch, and was usurping his throne.

Yet at the apogee of her glory Jeanne Du Barry would pass through moments of anguish. She realized that Louis was slowly but surely failing, and then!! She would be at the mercy of Louis XVI and his Queen Marie Antoinette. 'I am afraid of what awaits me,' she would say to Chon. Chon could find no comfort for her apprehensions.

9

A Year of Doubts

Louis XV was bored and lonely in the boudoir of Jeanne Du Barry. Each day the void around him increased, all those who had been the most assiduous in their attendance at Court had transferred their homage to the Choiseuls in exile. D'Aiguillon advised the King to punish all those who did not bother to ask his permission for their visits to Chanteloup. Louis answered, 'If I was younger I should feel angry, but at my age I want repose.'

The Diplomats acknowledged among themselves that the ruling power in France was the King's mistress, so they bowed down to the 'Goddess' and thus hoped to obtain their demands. It is a curious fact that although Jeanne was now besieged by the greater part of Europe, begging for her protection, she did not realize it, it did not really touch her inner self. She was a child of nature and accepted all this adulation as a natural consequence of her present existence. She helped those who asked for her benevolence, the Vienna Cabinet, the Kings of Prussia, of England, Gustave of Sweden. She helped them, as she had helped her companions of long ago, who had been less successful than herself in finding lovers to care for them. Even Mercy, the Austrian Envoy, confidant of the August Empress Marie-Therese, had fallen victim to the Du Barry's attractive omnipotence. Mercy hid this from Marie Antoinette, who still had addressed only eight words to the favourite. He wrote to the Empress, 'I see the Du Barry; it is absolutely obligatory that I should, she directs the King!!'

Louis XV was now sixty-four. Lent was approaching and once again the gnawing idea of the Pascal Communion was causing the

King his annual uneasiness. In reality he was a fervent believer and the dread of the hereafter would distress him at times. He had visited his daughter Madame Louise on several occasions. There he would find repose, they would discuss the life to come and in her great faith she would bid him to forsake the tie that kept him from grace, she would lead him to the lovely chapel, and father and daughter would pray before their God. He had obtained special permission to see her openly. Madame Du Barry became alarmed as these visits to the Convent of Saint Denis increased. She felt that the peril was greater than passing his time with some new amourette. He never spoke of these rendezvous. Richelieu confided to her, how often the King would now mention death, and add, 'I am getting old, will I have time to atone for all the wrongs of my existence?' To Jeanne these words would bring on a heart-sinking despondency, she realized that against the force of religion and the mysticism of faith there were no weapons.

In her austere cell Madame Louise was losing hope, she knew that the King, her father, could not cut the ropes which encircled his every limb. They had dug into his flesh, nothing could un-loosen them, but there was a way out, the only one possible, that he should marry his mistress. In that manner his life of sin would cease and his conscience would be appeased. Secretly she asked Maupeou to come to see her. Through the veiled grill of the Convent parlour she trusted him with her hope, 'You will work and I shall pray,' were her words as the Chancellor bowed low and the wooden window was closed. The Duc d'Aiguillon and Monsieur Maupeou had ceased their cordial relations, but this new scheme drew them together and they decided that before mentioning the King's union with his favourite, she must be divorced. Madame Louise in her emotional inspiration had for-gotten that important item.

Soon the rumour spread over Europe. Marie-Therese wrote to her envoy, 'It is said that Madame Louise, the Carmelite nun is negotiating with the Pope for the divorce of the favourite. To the prospect of Madame Du Barry becoming my daughter's grand-mother, I myself am indifferent, but I wish to know if it is true.'

The Ambassador answered, 'The Chancellor aided by the Arch-bishop of Paris is leading Madame Louise into difficult channels which she does not comprehend.' The interested person, Jeanne Du Barry, was bewildered. The King was not perturbed, Mesdames de France who did not know as yet Louise's idea still hoped that their father would marry some princess, Marie Antoinette did not allow the subject to be mentioned before her, Choiseul and the whole of Chanteloup were outraged. Maupeou, and the Abbé Terray were constantly visiting the proposed bride, and assuring her of success. One evening d'Aiguillon told the Monarch that a disagreeable rumour was spreading; it said that the Comte Guillaume Du Barry, Jeanne's husband, had been done away with by order of the highest authority. So strongly had this tale taken hold of the public that he advised that Guillaume Du Barry should be sent for and shown around, so as to destroy this unsavoury story. In a few days Guillaume arrived, fat and healthy. He was given a lump sum and told to go ahead and show himself every-where and lead a reckless life for some days so as to end this tale. Soon he found his way to his wife's abode and pestered her to obtain for him a huge pension. All this time Jean Du Barry had led a life of pleasure, although Jeanne had removed him entirely from her existence, there were times when he still assailed her for money. At last Guillaume, with well filled pockets, left the capital in which he had been seen by almost every inhabitant. The un-certainty of her future state and the knowledge that time was passing and nothing was settled was becoming a nightmare to Jeanne. She told Chon, 'If I marry Louis I shall have a stable position, now . . .' She did not end the sentence.

On several occasions lately the King had complained of fatigue, the excesses of his life had told on his strength. Only a few days ago he had confided to his doctor, 'I think I must limit my sensual activities.' 'I think,' responded the physician, 'that Your Majesty must end them.' Perhaps Madame Louise had touched a vital cord of his conscience, but he realized how weak his will had been against sin, and how often the fight between his senses and his soul had tortured him. How often he had longed for the things of heaven and yet his senses had thirsted for those of the flesh, and he had succumbed.

Unknown except to Chon, Jeanne was preparing to become Queen of France. With Chon's aid she was practising to attain a certain manner of haughtiness, of condescension, of benevolence; Chon had often witnessed Marie Leczinska's attitudes on public occasions. So with doors closed, before a large mirror Jeanne would rehearse the different ways of bowing in response to the courtiers' reverences. The famous modistes were crowding her boudoir, and losing themselves in the excitement of obeying her commands. So each day in her brilliant entourage Jeanne Du Barry hoped, each day in her cold cell a nun hoped, each day the hopes drifted further away. Then came the final great disappointment which submerged them all. The Archbishop announced after all possible procedure of finding a means of ending the union of the Comte and Comtesse Guillaume Du Barry, the answer had come from Rome – there could not be a divorce. That whole day and evening Jeanne smiled as usual and looked unconcerned, she knew only too well that the eyes of society were watching her every reaction for a sign of her disappointment. Louis XV told Richelieu, 'Nothing is changed, we shall continue as before.'

A new Parliament had been convened, the work of Maupeou – but too late, the Abbé Terray stood before an empty Treasury. To try and stem the utter ruin of the country taxes were imposed on the nobles, duties were being levied in all directions and on all the population. The Royal Princes had to sell some of their horses and reduce their way of living. As all classes were being affected the whole of France, high and low, cried out in their anger. The only one exempt from these drastic measures was Madame Du Barry. She had nothing to fear from the disagreeable new measures, which were ruining many people, the Royal Treasury, what was left of it, was opened for her benefit by order of Terray, her demands were accepted as coming from His Majesty. At this time the celebrated goldsmith, Roettiers de la Tour, was creating for her a gold dinner service chased with motifs of roses and myrtle leaves, at the same time he was completing her gold *toilette* set. Crowds would visit the artist's workshop examining each piece as it was finished. The mirror was a miracle of workmanship, surmounted by a crown supported by two cupids. Although enraptured in admiration for the work, the people were not blinded as to the expense involved, and because of their anger, which was almost turning it into a scandal, the jeweller had to cease working on the mirror.

The Marquise de Montrabé, alias Anne Becu, now lived in splendour, in the Convent of Sainte Elizabeth. Although residing in this holy place she owned a sumptuous apartment, and her staff was numerous, carriages, horses, sedan chairs awaited her caprice. Yet in her heart she had remained the cook of Francesca. She never came to Court, but Jeanne often went to her for consolation, when the existence she was leading suffocated her, there she would ever find a solace in her mother's arms. Then their joy would be to repair to a small kitchen, which Anne had had built for herself, they would dismiss all the grandeur and once again Anne would roll up her sleeves and revert to preparing her *pot-au-feu*. Jeanne would divest herself of her magnificent clothes and don a petticoat and apron which were kept for those occasions when together they would cook those mouthwatering dishes which they used to love and which reminded them of their vanished life of freedom. Only the King and Chon knew of these treasured escapades. One evening as they sat huddled together in the small space, Anne drew her child to her, and with tears in her eyes asked, 'Tell me Jeanne, are you happy?'

'*Non Maman*,' replied Jeanne, 'I am afraid.'

'But *ma chérie*, you have all the Court at your feet.'

'Yes,' replied Jeanne, 'but they can easily raise themselves and stab my heart.'

The philosophers, the devout, the politicians, the heads of states, one and all had their thoughts and fears centred on the woman who herself was beset with fear. Marie Antoinette by dint of advice from her mother had again addressed a few words to her. It had been during the sojourn at Fontainebleau, where it was the custom that at some part during the stay the ladies should offer their homage to the Dauphine. The Duchesse d'Aiguillon and Madame Du Barry, the latter trembling with apprehension, decided they must present themselves. Jeanne had asked Mercy's protection. As they made their reverence, the Dauphine, addressing herself to Madame Du Barry, said in a clear voice, 'It is bad weather today; one will not be able to take a walk.' That day at her audiences, Jeanne was overwhelmed; ladies bearing the highest names in France asked to be admitted. Some were refused admission. In reality Versailles was becoming a madhouse.

The philosophers were becoming bolder, many individuals were being drawn to the deism of Voltaire, yet they admitted a personal God of Vengeance. In their war against the Catholic religion the idealists such as Diderot, Jean-Jacques Rousseau, Montesquieu tried to extinguish the belief of centuries. The dogma of the Church, Paradise, Eve tempted by the serpent, original sin, were for Voltaire subjects of great ridicule, yet he confessed and received Holy Communion. These doctrines were penetrating further and further, Society was tickled by these new ideas, the *bourgeoisie* was interested, and the people awakened from their centuries of prayers. In a short time they would lose the stability of their faith and revolution would engulf them all.

Lent was approaching once again. The Comtesse Du Barry was waiting anxiously to see whether the King would take Holy Communion, if he did, her role was ended. To intensify her fears the vehement Abbé de Beauvais, Bishop of Senez, was to preach the Pascal retreat. On Holy Thursday he preached before His Majesty who sat alone: behind him was the Comtesse Du Barry, and behind her the whole Court. The Bishop was well known for his eloquence and above all for his dauntless courage in his zeal against sin. That day in the Chapel of Versailles he preached an extraordinary sermon, he seemed possessed with the fire of heaven, he denounced the vices of his audience in a voice which shook the very walls of the edifice. He ended by saying, 'Still forty days and "Nineveh" will be destroyed.' Later some of the Courtiers criticized the Bishop for his terrifying words. The King deeply impressed answered, 'This priest has only done his duty.'

The whole atmosphere of Versailles was altering. The King was listless, the death of several of those around him had affected his whole aspect on life. Jeanne was almost beside herself with fear of the future, she knew that those whom she considered her great allies were ready to betray her at the least sign of misfortune. Mercy writes to the Empress Marie-Therese, 'Lately I have discovered that there is a plot against the mistress. The Duc d'Aiguillon who owes his whole fortune to her is not pleased with her actual behaviour. She is capricious and inconsiderate towards him. All this might occasion new complications and new events.'

It was at this time that a new element came into Jeanne's life, but it had to be kept secret for fear of those she mistrusted. The Duc de Brissac, one of the most handsome men of the Court had captivated her. She had known him since her advent at the Court but they had rarely spoken to one another. During one of his visits to Versailles he had been given an apartment adjacent to hers, the inevitable happened. On account of his health, the King had rarely spent the night with her lately, so Jeanne considered herself free – although the utmost caution was necessary.

At last the dreaded Holy week was over, the King had not made his Easter Communion. Jeanne seemed to revive, she felt quieter, but she did not relax her constant surveillance on her entourage, as she was aware of the baseness of their plans. She had been told that a new candidate had been proposed for the post of the King's mistress – a handsome Dutch woman, the danger was imminent. In a curious letter written by a correspondent to Prince Dimitri Galitzyne, previous Russian Ambassador to the Court of France, are described the latest intrigues which were being woven around the Royal couch. It justified the anxiety of Madame Du Barry.

The Hague, 3rd of May 1774

'. . . Mon Prince, although peace seems to envelop us for the moment, friends have informed me that this apparent calm will be shattered by an unexpected event which will cause great surprise. It is the dismissal of the Comtesse Du Barry by order of the King's doctors, who have declared that she is too young for His Majesty. She will be sent to Spa this summer to take the waters. Meanwhile as a role like hers cannot be left empty, an older woman will replace her, a Dutch lady, Madame Neuwerkerke. She is an intimate of the Duc de Choiseul, who no doubt will return to power. D'Aiguillon, who is tolerated only on account of the Du Barry's friendship will be sent away.'

10

The Death of Louis XV

The *Almanach de Liège* announced among its prophesies for the year 1774, that during the month of April a lady holding a high position in one of the Foreign Courts would be exiled and during that same month a reigning Sovereign would fall dangerously ill, from which illness he would not recover. Jeanne who had read this, and was highly superstitious like all women of her class, was tormented by a vague uneasiness, constantly she murmured, 'I wish that foreboding month of April was over!'[1]

The month of April was nearly spent, Jeanne's fears were fading. The King desired to spend a few days at his beloved Trianon. He wanted to be alone with Jeanne away from the tumult which people were creating in the hope of directing his life.

That evening of the 26th of April 1774 was never to be forgotten by the Du Barry. Trianon looked enchanting with its orgy of spring flowers tumbling and embracing one another in a riot of colour. The King and she reclined on a sofa, one of those gilded ornamental pieces of the period. Although it was early spring the windows had been left open, no sound except the birds saying their evening prayers to God. She felt relieved; only four more days to the end of the dreaded month! Louis was especially loving, he drew her to him and touchingly spoke of the future, 'As long as I live you will be the only lovely one to fill my heart.' So all anxieties slipped away. Later in the days of her solitude, Trianon that night and, above all, her security in Louis XV's arms would overwhelm her with the enchantment of the past.

Fear of smallpox was a constant torment. At the slightest sign

[1] Edmond et Jules de Goncourt – *La Du Barry*.

of illness the sick and their families would immediately imagine the threat of that scourge. Vaccination had recently been introduced but people were beset by indecision as to whether to risk it. Those who did were considered heroes or madmen. The Comte de Cheverny who was the Introducteur des Ambassadeurs tells us the routine which had to be followed when inoculation took place. The Parliaments had decreed that no inoculation could take place in the capital and that it had to be done in the country, in a house which would have to be pulled down immediately after the quarantine period was over, whether the inoculation had been successful or not. For three weeks before the event physicians prescribed a diet of chicken only, rabbit and spinach cooked in water, and no wine, the patients had also to be purged three times a week. When the Comte de Cheverny was inoculated the whole affair was given great publicity. He tells us, 'A week later I had an attack of fever which developed into severe smallpox, from which I nearly died!' As he was one of the important officials of the Court the result of his inoculation for a time frightened people. The King was not inoculated!

As his valet drew back the curtains on the 27th of April the King complained of feeling unwell; at the same time he told him to fetch Madame la Comtesse for by order of the doctors they had been sleeping apart. When she came to him, he told her that his whole body was in pain, he had lain awake for hours. She was struck by his looks, she asked him to send for his doctor. 'No,' he replied, 'I will not miss following the hunt this evening, but I shall do so in a coach. If I see the doctor he will forbid it.' During the hunt Jeanne noticed, he was in great suffering. On his return Louis XV shut himself away in his rooms alone with Jeanne. She remembered the prophesy.

Alone with him, all the doors locked for fear of intruders, she felt distraught, she tried to soothe him, but the pain kept increasing and still by a strange obstinacy he continued to refuse to see his doctor. Late in the night Jeanne was allowed to send for his physician, Lemonnier, the King's chief doctor who had cared for

The Death of Louis XV

His Majesty for years; he did not seem anxious nor did he antici-
pate a serious illness. Louis insisted that only Jeanne, his valet,
and Doctor Lemonnier should nurse him. At three o'clock the
Ministers arrived from Paris. Discussions were started whether
the King should remain at Trianon or be transported back to
Versailles in case of a grave illness. Mesdames de France, the
Dauphin and Dauphine arrived and made more suggestions which
added to the general bewilderment. Still Louis refused to see any
of them. At last the Royal chief surgeon was summoned, on seeing
the state of the King he did not hesitate, but ordered the immediate departure for Versailles.

Louis XV was once again and for the last time in the abode he
loved. By now most of the renowned doctors had examined him
but none could diagnose the malady. The news of the King's illness had reached the capital. Once again the road leading to the
château was filled with traffic. Some of this crowd had rushed to
Versailles to be in the midst of the excitement, others with a true
sense of loyalty to be near their Monarch in his sufferings.

The illness was progressing, the doctors suggested that the
King should be bled but Lemonnier was opposed to this measure
and it was postponed until the next day. That night the King's
fever increased, he had hallucinations, and cried out for Madame
de Pompadour; the doctors, there were several, requested Madame
Du Barry to keep away.

The next day the King was worse, yet the etiquette was such
that the Officers on guard had approached his bed to accept the
pass word. As His Majesty gave it the Officers were scared, he was
almost unrecognizable.

That night the King seemed more lucid, his valet was near him
in case of need, his voice was harsh as he bade him fetch Madame
la Comtesse. At the same time, since many courtiers had crowded
into the room, he told Lemonnier, 'Send all these people away, I
wish to be alone with Madame Du Barry.' For an hour they were
together, no one dared to disturb them. As she bade him good
night she shivered, had he prepared her for the worst?

On the 30th of April the King was bled twice. He was desperately weak, and asked for his daughters and the Dauphin and Dauphine. They came but he did not speak to them, they were alarmed. Later in the evening, as the light was fading, Lemonnier took up a candle to examine his patient. As he bent over him he detected red spots; he brought the lighted taper nearer, the pimples were already forming, no doubt remained – it was the smallpox! The order went forth, on no account was the King to be told. Without a moment's dread of contagion, Madame Adelaide, Madame Victoire and Madame Sophie decided to tend their father in his every requirement. So the routine began. Once they had ended their day's work, Jeanne would quietly slip into the infected room and take up her vigil. Everyone seemed relieved, after all smallpox could be cured, and His Majesty was surrounded by such clever doctors, surely he would be saved! The Comte de Cheverny tells us in his memoirs that Doctor Lorry, one of the doctors tending the King, met a friend of his and told him that whilst others were relieved that His Majesty was better, and were chanting victory, he believed the King would continue to improve until the 11th, then would take a turn for the worse, and on the 13th he would cease to exist. Although Doctor Lorry had begged that his forecast should not be divulged, the Comte de Cheverny learned of it and immediately realized the seriousness of the communication. He wrote: 'I drove straight to the Lieutenant of Police, who was already in bed. As I was known I was admitted, I told him what I had just heard, we sat for an hour discussing the regulations which the King's death would entail.'

During these morbid days endless arguments were being carried on, Mesdames were agitating to save their father's soul. They were arguing that the Archbishop must be sent for to confess him. The Archbishop had already come to pay a visit, but Richelieu had asked him politely to leave, saying that seeing him would kill the King, who would realize that his last hour had come. The two factions were in open hostilities, they talked loudly, at times their angry remonstrations took place in Louis XV's room. Jeanne heard it all and was helpless; she knew that his confession would mean the end of her life near Louis. On the 4th of May, the King seemed less drowsy, he was idly looking at his hands when the terrible realization dawned, he gave one cry, 'It is smallpox, yes I have smallpox!' No one broke the silence, he had recognized the dreadful spots. The rest of that day he spoke little, and lay awake seemingly in deep thought. Richelieu watched him, Mesdames de France also watched and wondered. In the convent of St. Denis the nuns were beseeching God to save his life. It was almost eleven o'clock, Jeanne was preparing all that would be required for the nightly vigil. The attendants had retired, she was alone and thought the King was asleep, so she worked noiselessly, then he called her name, he could hardly see, his face had lost all human shape. Her heart sank with pity, gently with her lovely fingers she soothed his swollen putrid brow. She felt only sorry for him, no repugnance for this distorted effigy of a man who once had been so beautiful. Gently he lowered her hand and held it, and in a faint voice told her, 'Now that I am aware of my illness we must not recommence the scandal of Metz. If I had known before what I know now, I should never have allowed you to come to me.[1] Now I owe myself to Almighty God, and to my subjects, so you must leave me and retire from Versailles tomorrow morning, tell d'Aiguillon to come to me tomorrow morning at ten o'clock.' She glanced at the clock, it was midnight, she slowly withdrew her hand from his and walked to the table where all the medicines stood, and prepared the potion to be given at this time; all night she continued her task of nursing. The King did not speak to her again. As dawn was breaking she was relieved of her duties by Doctor Lemonnier. As she left the room of the dying King she looked once more at her lover, his eyes were closed, was he asleep – she never knew!

On the 5th of May when d'Aiguillon entered the King's room at ten o'clock he was almost forced to withdraw. Although the

[1] The King was alluding to the fact that during the Austrian war of succession in 1744 he had fallen dangerously ill in Metz, and had been persuaded to repudiate Madame de Châteauroux. When he improved she had returned which had caused a great scandal at the time.

windows were slightly opened the stench was nauseating, and yet Jeanne Du Barry, under the King's order of dismissal had tended him and endured the foulness of the air. Louis XV told the Duc to arrange for the Comtesse's departure and asked him to take her to the Duc's château at Rueil. At four o'clock the Comtesse Du Barry, accompanied by Chon and the Duchesse d'Aiguillon, left Versailles for ever, on her way to Rueil. At six o'clock Louis asked for his valet La Borde, then as usual told him to fetch Madame la Comtesse! La Borde replied, 'Sire, she has already left.'

'Where has she gone?'

'To Rueil, Sire.'

'Oh! already!'

Then Louis turned on his side and buried his face in his covers, La Borde had time to perceive two large tears coursing down the King's face.

'His Majesty, if possible, was worse.' Such was the bulletin sent forth the next morning. Masses, prayers, the forty hours devotion were being said in all the churches, but still Louis did not ask for a priest, and no one dared interrupt his silence. The dread of contagion was affecting the minds of the courtiers and yet they remained in the infected atmosphere for fear of missing the opportunity to pay homage to the new King on his accession, which they calculated must be imminent. The King was fully conscious but in great pain, Mesdames de France were frantic, the hours were passing and yet no question of confession. The whole of France was waiting for the King's death!!

The 7th of May. Will he survive this day? The avenues leading to the château as well as the whole square before the gates were crowded with a multitude of people. Some were making a holiday of the day, others found that the Sovereign was taking a long time to die. Inside the château the strain was tense, what a scandal if the King expired without repenting for his licentious past existence! In the King's room there was no sound except for the laboured breathing of the patient. Then he spoke, 'Ask the Abbé Maudoux to come to me.' Alone with his confessor, the Monarch who had dominated the world by his splendour, who had stood on the

Versailles – corner of a room in 'Les Petits Appartements de Madame Du Barry'

Louis Hercule Timoléon de Cossé, Duc de Brissac, French
School c. 1780

pinnacle of power, now with great humility begged for forgiveness of his God, for the evil he had committed during his long life. The Abbé was absolving him, when a message was brought to the priest from the Cardinal de la Roche-Aymon, that in view of the important position and notoriety of his past life of scandal, the King must atone publicly before receiving absolution. Although very weak the King consented. When the Cardinal arrived the King asked him to read his public confession for him. The rooms, the hall, the corridors, the stairways were crammed with people of all ranks but nobody spoke, the silence was oppressive. The doors of the King's rooms opened, people pressed forward, the Cardinal in all his display appeared. He raised his hand and spoke, 'His Majesty Louis XV has confessed his sins to Almighty God, and now he wishes to atone publicly to his subjects and to the world. His Majesty has commanded me, his humble servant, to speak on his behalf, he has asked Almighty God to pardon his offences and the scandalous example he has set his people during his reign. Should Almighty God vouchsafe to grant him health he will devote the remainder of his life to repentance, to the support of religion and the good of his subjects. Amen!'

Three days later it was still dark as the bodyguard, the Swiss Guard, lined the whole way from the church and formed into a mighty procession to escort the blessed host which was being taken to His Majesty Louis XV. It was an imposing sight, the Cardinal de la Roche-Aymon in his robes holding aloft the covered Chalice, the poles of the canopy held by high ranking priests in their silver and gold copes, followed by numerous others carrying lighted tapers. Walking behind them the Dauphin and the Dauphine and the rest of the Royal Family equally holding lighted tapers. The Cardinal with bowed head prayed silently but the rest of the long procession chanted prayers for the dying. As it reached the first steps of the grand staircase the Dauphin and Dauphine and the members of the Royal Family, except Mesdames, withdrew on account of the infection. On reaching the King's room only the Cardinal and a few of the priests entered, and in the silence of that infested room Louis XV received Holy

Communion and extreme unction. He was conscious and although unable to recite the answers to the prayers for the dying, he followed every word in a most holy attitude. The scene was moving, he had been laid on his camp bed, the curtains had been drawn back, the room was lit vividly by the quantities of tapers held by priests kneeling around the bed. The King was motionless, his mouth was partly opened, his face showed no trepidation, it resembled the head of a Moor, a head of bronze! At one o'clock during the agony the King was still conscious, the Abbé Maudoux asked him if he was suffering. 'Ah! ah! ah! very much.' Those three cries expressed the terrible torture he was experiencing, then the King murmured, 'My body is in torture, but my soul is at peace.' The Abbé later declared, that he hoped his own death would be as holy as the passing of Louis XV.

At 3.15 the King was no more. At 3.17 the doors were thrown open and the Duc de Bouillon, Grand Chamberlain came forth from the King's room and announced in a voice of thunder, so as to be heard by all, 'Messieurs, the King is dead. Long live the King!' When the news reached Rueil, the Comtesse Du Barry retired to her room and refused to see anyone that evening.

The King had asked that his funeral should take place as simply as possible. Monsieur de Sartines, Chief of the Police, feared the attitude of the mob; so many disloyal speeches had been made against the late King. It was decided that the convoy to St. Denis would proceed late in the evening. On the 12th of May at ten o'clock at night the hearse left Versailles, the King was being taken to the Abbey where he would crumble into dust, the fate of the lovely Marquise de Pompadour a decade ago. Most of the Royal Family had already left Versailles, etiquette forbade them to remain in any abode where a dead person lay. Most of the Courtiers had also left, it was no longer necessary to pay homage to Louis XV. So at ten o'clock in the gloom of night the convoy got under way. The Monarch's body was escorted by three hundred *Gardes du Corps*, and Cavalry men carrying torches surrounded the hearse, the horses were made to canter, passing swiftly along the road to avoid disagreeable scenes. On arriving at

St. Denis the mob who had waited broke into jeers and shouts of derision, singing, '*Voilà le plaisir des dames. Voici leur délice.*' (Here comes the ladies' pleasure. Here comes the ladies' delight.) The mob, losing all restraint, tried to assault the bier, but they were too late, the cortège had already been engulfed in the dark courts of the Abbey. Until late the multitude sang and hooted, insulting the Monarch they once had named 'The Beloved'.

11

Du Barry a Prisoner

That same night at ten o'clock, the Comtesse Du Barry was taken prisoner and escorted in her coach by armed soldiers to the state Abbey of Pont-aux-Dames. During that long drive she was alone in utter darkness. Now and then she would catch a glimpse of the road, as one of the escorts carrying a torch would pass by the window. It had been but an hour previous that a company of soldiers had come to Rueil to fetch her. At first she did not comprehend what they meant. So brutally they had told her, 'We have been commanded to arrest you and to take you to be interned.' They had ordered her to hurry. Seeing her maid she had bade her pack some clothes, 'No need for that,' said the young commander, 'Take a nightgown, that will suffice. You will get prisoner's clothes when you get there.' She had asked if her maid could accompany her, they had laughed and had taken her by the arm and dragged her to the coach. She sat shivering in the obscurity.

She knew that Louis was being buried at that moment, in her despair she wondered which of the two of them was the more to be pitied. At last the coach pulled up with a jerk on the uneven stones, they had arrived at the entrance to the Abbey of Pont-aux-Dames. The escorts had gathered around the courtyard and she could barely discern the high walls of the severe building. The massive doors of the prison opened and she was told to enter. As she stood in the dilapidated hall, in a flash she remembered the Convent of the Daughters of Ste. Aure where for seven years she had survived. Presently an inner door opened and the Abbess, Madame de la Roche-Fontenelle accompanied by the community appeared, all in a state of suppressed excitement. They had been told the name of the new prisoner, for them it was the devil in disguise which had come among them. The young nuns had been warned to keep away from her, but even the rigid Abbess sustained a shock when this lovely creature appeared before her. Jeanne was led into the remotest part of the building and left by herself, she had never seen such a forlorn spot, the walls were made of grey stone, a small hole deep in the wall, she surmised, would just let pass a ray of light. No curtains, a few strands of straw laid sparsely on the floor, a wooden table, a wooden chair, a low bed with a straw mattress and one blanket; in a corner hung a dim lantern, but overshadowing all this hung a huge crucifix over the door with one word, 'REPENT'. Her eyes became progressively accustomed to the dimness, and as the horror of the cell in which she was to live gradually revealed itself, in her misery she cried out, 'No, not here, not here!'

Presently the heavy door opened and an elderly nun appeared bringing a bowl of soup and a loaf of bread, she laid these on the rickety table and fished out a spoon from her large pocket. She looked at Jeanne, a look of extreme pity – she knew! With a kind voice she said, '*Ma petite*, you are still very young, do not be frightened, all this will pass and you will be happy but only for a time. But remember whatever is in store never despair, this life is only a moment of transition, I shall pray to God to protect you.' Jeanne ate her soup and lay down on her straw palliasse, she felt calmer, the old nun had promised to pray for her. Next morning the same aged nun, *soeur* Angélique, brought in a bundle of clothes – the prison uniform. She told Jeanne she would have to wear it, it consisted of a thick rough chemise, an equally thick and rough petticoat, a grey woollen dress and the traditional prison hood.

The days passed, Jeanne lost account of time. Now and then one of the older nuns would come to look at her. Even the formidable Abbess would venture into that cold cell and inquire how she was faring. To their astonishment she did not complain but received them with a sad smile. Sister Angélique had told the community how different she was from what they had imagined. One morning the Abbess entered her cell earlier than usual, told her the weather was fine and asked if she would like to take a walk in the garden. From that moment Jeanne spent a great deal of the time with the nuns. She would make herself useful in the kitchen, teach them new dishes and help them in their menial tasks. The nuns were finding her enchanting, they forgot that she had been branded as the most immoral woman in France. They forgot that she was a State prisoner, they saw only that she was a woman who had possessed all that wealth could bring and did not resent adversity.

Marie Antoinette's hatred of the Du Barry had not abated. In a letter to the Empress Marie-Therese, her mother, she wrote, 'The creature has been imprisoned in a convent and everyone connected with that scandal has been hounded out of Court.'

The Empress wrote to Count Mercy, 'I have received a heartless letter from my daughter, in which she alludes to the poor Du Barry as that "creature". In my answer I have pointed out that this miserable woman is more to be pitied than anyone. She has lost everything, she has no consolation, no resources, no real religion, which in these terrible circumstances is the only solace.' In those first days of tragedy Marie-Therese was the only one to express pity for her.

Gradually news filtered through the prison walls and Jeanne heard that d'Aiguillon, the Abbé Terray and Maupeou had been deposed. The new Prime Minister had been named, it was Monsieur de Maurepas, a witty and easy-going nobleman she had known in the old days, she hoped he would help her. She heard he was inhabiting a part of the apartment she had occupied at Versailles. A letter was handed to her, the only one she had received so far. It came from a very humble young man, whom out of compassion she had engaged as a librarian in Louveciennes. It read:

'Madame la Comtesse,

I humbly beg your forgiveness for presuming to address you, but I thought that you might like to have news of your mother

Madame la Marquise de Montrabé. So I ventured to ask to be received by her. I found her very sad. Please if it is in your power, give her news of yourself as often as possible. I also passed an hour with Monsieur La Borde, who is very afflicted. He asked me to let you know that he will always be at your command. Directly it is allowed I shall travel to Louveciennes and inspect the library.

Your respectful and humble servant,

Desfontaines.'

Jeanne Du Barry was not unhappy, the nuns seemed to have accepted her as a friend. The stern Abbess was slowly unbending, the whole community, choir-Mothers, and lay Sisters were captivated by her charm and her gentleness. The daily mass, the frequent prayers, the serenity permeating the very walls made her forget her ugly surroundings. All this was bringing peace to her tormented soul. The world she had lived in was now remote. Then her tranquillity was shattered, her creditors – there were many – discovered her retreat. The sums she owed were very great.

She had hoped that they would consider her position, as for the moment she had no resources, and no knowledge of where her jewels had been taken. She was in total ignorance as to whether Louveciennes and the different sources of her income still belonged to her, or whether they had been confiscated. The Abbess advised her to ask permission for a lawyer to come and discuss ways and means of settling her debts. This was granted. As the whole affair was very involved, her intendant, Montvallier, and Aubert, the Crown Jeweller, were given leave to see her.

If they still belonged to her, the Comtesse declared she was quite willing to part with some of her treasures, her magnificent emerald set, some of her famous pictures and furniture at Louveciennes, as she was determined that all debts would be honoured. She also desired that the salaries and wages of her numerous staff should be given them. She made a list of the servants she intended to keep and those she wished to be dismissed. Here is part of the order she wrote:

'I the undersigned authorize Monsieur Aubert to conclude the sale of my formal bodice set in diamonds, which consists of a stomacher, epaulettes and a brooch in the shape of a bow. I also authorize him to conclude the sale of my set of rubies and diamonds, etc. . . .'

Although these jewels were sold, she still possessed a fortune in jewellery.

Life seemed to stand still in the surroundings in which she was living. Her natural instincts commenced to revive, she told herself, 'I am still young,' and as she looked into a small mirror, which she had smuggled from Rueil, 'Still lovely!' These long months of utter isolation from all that she had known had been a balm to the bitterness of her distress. The Abbess and Jeanne had become true friends, this friendship lasted twenty years. The Abbess wrote to the Prime Minister asking for the release of her prisoner, on the plea of her ill health. This letter was put before Louis XVI, who answered, 'No.'

Several friends of Jeanne pleaded trying to soften the King's decision. Monsieur de Maurepas, the Prince de Ligne, the Duc de La Vrillière interceded for her liberation, but Louis XVI urged by the obstinacy of Marie Antoinette turned down all these demands. In the meantime the good Sisters tended Jeanne with love and devotion, trying to lighten her burden. At last the Prince de Ligne approached the Queen and with his eloquence succeeded in obtaining permission for Madame Du Barry to walk in the park of the Convent. The peasants came to the gates of the prison and she would distribute small gifts to them. They never forgot her charming manner and much later when they learned of her tragedy they sincerely lamented, and remembered her generosity.

On the 25th of May 1775 the Prince de Ligne was told that Madame Du Barry was now allowed to go out of the Convent's grounds, and walk about the countryside, on the condition that she regained Pont-aux-Dames to sleep. A month later she was given her freedom, but she was not allowed to reside nearer than ten miles distance from the Court or capital. At once her thoughts reverted to Louveciennes. Alas! It was too near Versailles. She asked her intendant to purchase a property for her within the prescribed limits. The Château de Saint-Vrain became her new residence. Although she was entranced with joy at possessing a home once again, it was with great regret that she parted from all her dear nuns – they were in tears. She promised to return to see them, they could not be consoled. When the moment of departure was imminent, the holy Abbess and the great sinner knelt alone in the empty chapel, the Abbess rose from her knees and blessed the woman she had learned to admire, she put into her hands a rosary, it was found after the Du Barry's death at Louveciennes. The Comtesse Du Barry left her prison, twenty years of freedom lay before her!

12

Return to Louveciennes

The Château de Saint-Vrain was a vast construction surrounded by a moat, whose waters culminated in a picturesque lake. Madame Du Barry knew the property; by a strange coincidence it had belonged to the second son of Madame de la Garde, the elderly lady whom she had once served as lady's maid. She had been dismissed ignominiously, when her liaison with this young man had been discovered. The house was very handsome, but had a solemn sadness about it, how different from her beloved Louveciennes. The Duc d'Aiguillon had advanced the needed sum for its acquisition. It cost two hundred thousand livres, plus fifteen thousand livres for the furniture. The contract had been signed at Pont-aux-Dames on the 9th of April 1775. At once she recalled her servants, she hoped to reconstruct the life that she had lost. She felt that the eyes of Versailles were watching her movements. So at first she modestly invited a few country neighbours to supper, and equally unassumingly she visited the needy in the village and supplied them with what they lacked. A few of her old friends courageously came to see her, among them the Duc d'Aiguillon who was still Commander of the King's Guard. Life was quiet, but Jeanne was not content. Saint-Vrain was too vast, soulless, immaterial. During her forced sojourn at Pont-aux-Dames she had had to submit to the rules but now that she was away from those restrictions her own nature revived. All those months her nature had been subdued, but now her senses revived and the old clamour for admiration and love with all its attraction was overwhelming her, she knew that she would never regain her equilibrium in the château. The one man with whom she longed to renew her liaison was the Duc de Brissac. They both knew that their meeting just now was an impossibility, he was Governor of Paris, and one of the King's most influential officials and she disgraced. Yet in a subtle manner he had kept her informed of his faithful devotion and unfailing adoration.

Lately more creditors had appeared, and once again Jeanne was harassed by financial worries. She had vowed to herself so often that henceforth she would curb her prodigal ways, and settle all her debts; but Jeanne Du Barry was a woman of purple and fine linen, although this necessity had lain dormant for over a year, when imprisoned. She was like those women, they are the exception, who bow down to the inevitable without a murmur, to revert to their true nature when events become normal. Each morning she would pledge her word of honour that she would abstain from any reckless expenditure on that day. Before the hour of dinner had arrived a host of different tempters would have presented their enticing wares and Jeanne, her eyes glistening with excitement would purchase for thousands of livres, oblivious of the cost. The pressure of the claimants became alarming. She sent for her lawyer and asked him to draw up a list of some of her finest pictures at Louveciennes and to dispose of them. At the same time she instructed him to put up for sale her magnificent mansion at Versailles in the Avenue de Paris. It was a gift from Louis XV who had said, 'When I die you will have to leave the château, so you will be assured of a home.' This mansion was bought by the Comte de Provence, later Louis XVIII. The proceeds from this transaction were sufficient to quieten her creditors, and with the residue of the sale she decided to buy a property for her mother, who had left the Convent of Ste. Elizabeth after the death of Louis XV. Jeanne hoped that the ban on her place of residence would be lifted, and she would be able to return to Louveciennes. In September 1775 the former Anne Rançon installed herself in the Maison Rouge. The château, situated near Villiers-sur-Orge, the gift of her daughter, stood in the midst of a large enclosed park. It contained innumerable buildings, a chapel, stables, glass houses, cottages. Monsieur Rançon had refused to follow his wife, derisively saying, 'My wife has become Madame la

Marquise, and my stepdaughter has just ceased being *Madame la Grande Favorite*, I remain what I am, *le père* Rançon.'

The contract for the disposal of her mansion in Versailles was to be signed at Louveciennes, and as the Court was in residence at Fontainebleau, she was allowed to spend a few hours in her lovely abode. As she walked into each room her heart rejoiced, all was just as she had left it. Someone with a depth of devotion must have watched over her treasures – she wondered, who? Young Desfontaines stood silent, her joy was his greatest reward. Jeanne felt that this permission to visit Louveciennes would lead to her complete freedom of movement.

The Prime Minister, the Comte de Maurepas, had obtained permission from Louis XVI to grant the Comtesse Du Barry her past revenues, her shares of the port of Nantes and those of the Hôtel de Ville, a total income of 145,000 livres. Also the life interest in Louveciennes, with its wealth which included the treasures from her apartment at Versailles. All that these rooms had contained which belonged to her had been taken to Louveciennes on the day she had been transferred to Pont-aux-Dames, this was apart from personal wealth valued at two million livres, in gold and jewels.

On the 6th of October Louveciennes was *en fête*. A message had come through, 'The Comtesse Du Barry has been allowed to return.' Two years of yearning for her home had drifted by, Jeanne was once more entering her lost paradise, Chon had returned and stood at the head of Jeanne's numerous staff, all ready to greet her. In the back row Desfontaines looked on unnoticed.

The Duc de Choiseul's hatred for the Du Barry had not abated after the death of Louis XV. He was certain that Louis XVI's first act would be to recall him and offer him the post of Prime Minister, but although Marie Antoinette pleaded for his return to office, the King refused. Choiseul's exile was ended, but so was his career. His resentment fell on the Comtesse, she was the 'alpha and omega' of his disgrace.

Return to Louveciennes

Notwithstanding the huge sums of money she had spent in settling her debts, Madame Du Barry had still enormous wealth at her disposal. All her love of luxury was coming back to her, and Louveciennes was becoming the show place of France. For illustrious foreigners it was considered obligatory to visit Madame Du Barry's home.

About this time a thunderbolt struck the Comtesse Du Barry and re-echoed all over France. A pamphlet published and printed in England appeared, called 'Les Anecdotes sur Madame la Comtesse Du Barry'. It was so scandalous and stinging that the Minister of the King's Household informed the Lieutenant of Police that it was advisable to employ every method to prevent the pamphlet from appearing in France. The author, Pidansat de Mayrobert, a secretary of the Duc de Chartres and coming from the lower class, had passed his life in antechambers, and was totally ignorant of the life at Court. This man evidently needed money, so he waited until Jeanne's protector was no longer alive, and she was defenceless. He poured out a torrent of untruths. Despite the efforts of suppression, a great many of these leaflets had already been sold in France, yet so unbelievably crude were they that even her most bitter enemies threw them aside.

13

The Duc de Brissac

The Queen, enchantingly capricious in her love of amusement, and surrounded by those whose only occupation was to lead her on in a round of pleasure, often ending in scenes of dissipation, was beginning to be secretly criticized. The criticism reached Vienna, and the Empress Marie-Therese became anxious. In the depth of her heart she knew where the real reason of her daughter's loss of dignity lay. It was seven years that she had lived with her husband, yet the marriage had not been consummated. The Empress resolved that the Emperor Joseph II, her son, should travel to France and endeavour to persuade Louis XVI to undergo a benign operation which would enable him to produce an heir.

The Emperor Joseph II of Austria arrived in the French capital. Society had made great preparations to receive him. Receptions, official dinner-parties, entertainments for his amusement were organized. The only one who dreaded his visit was his sister the Queen, she knew he would bring all her mother's remonstrances, and she realized that they were deserved. To everyone's astonishment the Emperor refused all invitations, he had come to dictate to his sister and when that was accomplished he intended to amuse himself as he alone understood enjoyment. He passed two days preaching to Marie Antoinette, and exhorting the King to be operated on. He finally persuaded Louis XVI to submit to this rather disagreeable experience. The Queen listened, and promised! Alas! The promises did not impress themselves unduly on her heart. The third day, having fulfilled his duty the Emperor determined to devote himself seriously to pleasure. He had heard so much of Madame Du Barry, so with the pretended excuse of viewing the Pavillon of Louveciennes, he asked to be allowed to visit her.

The Duc de Brissac

The Emperor Joseph II was travelling under the name of Count Falkenstein, and it was this title that he used when asking permission to visit Louveciennes. In reality the property meant little to him, but he was intrigued to meet the woman who had scandalized Europe. When his coach drew up at the front entrance of the château, Madame Du Barry came down the steps to greet him; with dignity she made a low reverence and together they entered the lovely hall. Making him pass before her she showed him into the large drawing-room. There they remained alone talking for two hours. The Emperor's aides-de-camps who had accompanied him were waiting impatiently, anxiously looking at the time. His Majesty had an important official dinner that night, and it was growing late. At length the doors opened and Madame Du Barry and her august guest appeared. How pretty Jeanne still was, although now thirty-four years old, perhaps a little less flamboyant, but infinitely more beautiful. As she stood smiling at the Emperor's gentlemen, who were saluting her, tears glistened in her eyes, was it the remembrance of another Monarch and other times? This woman who possessed every material thing in life and yet as Marie-Therese had written to her daughter 'had nothing'. Regardless of the distressed look of his gentlemen, His Majesty said, 'Messieurs, I charge you to return to Paris, and present my excuses to my hostess of this evening. Madame la Comtesse has offered to show me the pavilion and her gardens, I shall return later.' Then with great gallantry he offered her his arm, but the Du Barry withdrew and with a low curtsy said, 'Sire, I am not worthy of such an honour.' The Emperor gently drawing her arm through his said, 'Madame, remember beauty is always queen.'

When this visit became known it created a surge with mixed emotions. Marie Antoinette was furious, Louis XVI did not care, Maurepas was delighted, Marie-Therese thought it useless, but the man most offended was Choiseul. He had expected the Emperor to stop at Chanteloup on the day of his return to Austria, to partake of a magnificent repast, which had been prepared in his honour. Alas! The Emperor still under the charm of the Comtesse Du Barry declined to visit any other estate. When he drove straight past Chanteloup, Choiseul was in a paroxysm of fury. Thus the only person Joseph II had deigned to visit was that shameless dissolute demon in human shape.

The Emperor's visit had taken place just when Madame Du Barry needed a helping hand. Although the anecdotes were considered too vile to be noticed, many people had bought up the leaflets which had filtered through from England, and had gloated over their filth. Now the Imperial visitor had regilded the tarnished lustre of her name.

Gradually Jeanne's position assumed a definite standing, men who had known and admired her when she swayed Versailles found their way to Louveciennes. They knew it would be badly viewed by the Queen, but for some time the courtiers had seemed less obsequious. Was it the independence which would soon master France? Amongst them the Duc de Brissac resumed his intimate visits to Jeanne and love renewed its strong ties. The Duc de Brissac was a peer of the realm, Governor of Paris, and Lieutenant-Colonel of the hundred Swiss Guards. In 1760 he had married Diane, second daughter of the Duc de Nivernais. Grand *seigneur* of noble manner and an accomplished courtier, handsome, tall, fair haired and with fine blue eyes. Although he was in love with Jeanne, it did not prevent his having escapades with other women, but they never lasted long. For him no one could compare with Jeanne Du Barry. She had given herself to him at first as she had done to so many men, but apart from the sensual thrill which he brought to her, a strong attachment made her cling to him. He enraptured her being, he created a feeling which she had never experienced before, a feeling akin to possessing a husband. He was enormously wealthy, owned several estates and a palace in Paris. Now he had returned to her side and was constantly at Louveciennes trying to discover and satisfy her smallest need, they made an ideal pair. One day as they had stood together in the presence of a great painter, the latter had exclaimed, 'You would make Apollo and Venus shrink with envy.'

The Duchesse de Brissac had no objection to her husband's love affair with Madame Du Barry. She was aware of the Comtesse's

Madame Du Barry by Madame Vigée-Lebrun

frequent visits to their Paris residence and that her apartment adjoined the Duc's. Yet she refused to meet her saying that her husband's mistress might slumber under the same roof as herself, but on no account would she tolerate her using the same staircase. So Brissac had a small one made leading from Jeanne's room to a magnificent flight of steps for his mistress to ascend and descend when she resided at the palace.

The Emperor Joseph II had come and gone. Louis XVI had submitted to the operation, and Marie Antoinette had informed the Empress, 'Louis is normal, and we are now husband and wife.' But the impression her brother had made on her was fast being erased, all the admonitions and warnings to lead a more dignified life were soon put out of mind. The Comtesse de Noailles, her Grande Maitresse, nicknamed 'Madame Etiquette', deplored the Queen's mode of life. The Queen was a child at heart, and just like a child wanted to play. Masked balls were in great favour, as were the rural amusements at Trianon, where in dairymaids' costumes, she, and Princesse de Polignac, the woman she had taken to her heart, enacted the pastoral life of the country peasants. The extravagance she lavished on this friend and her family later formed one of the main charges at her trial.

Marie Antoinette was now the cynosure of Europe. Her gowns were designed by an artist, Madame Bertin. They were created in closed rooms, no stranger was allowed into the ateliers, and the seamstresses were sworn to secrecy. She was the leader of any new fashion, young, lively and beautiful, she loved gambling and flirtations. She did no harm, and no open scandal touched her reputation. A few names, such as the Duc de Lauzun and Count Fersen were linked with hers, but these were all guesses.

Perfect happiness is a myth, one rarely if ever experiences it! Only in later life one has the illusion that at a certain time one possessed it. Jeanne Du Barry in the worldly sense had acquired all she desired, riches, a certain position of respectability, which dimmed her past, a devoted lover. Yet her heart and mind were yearning for Versailles and for the Queen's recognition. When the

Duc de Brissac after a sojourn at Court, returned to her, he would naturally report all the gossip, Jeanne would shrink within herself and feel a pariah. She was not envious of Marie Antoinette, she even felt an affection for her; it was the Queen's disdain which still humiliated her. She longed to warn the Sovereign of the dangerous tales circulating within the country. She realized that the Queen did not know of the peril, she was young and rarely heard the truth, only flattery and approval were laid at her feet by those who aspired to obtain her favour. In a different manner Jeanne had had to parry many thrusts in her insecure elevation; sufferings, emotions, temptations, rarely allowing herself to indulge her whims. Would Marie Antoinette learn this inexorable rule before it was too late?

Among the merchants who daily flocked to Louveciennes were several jewellers who, well acquainted with the whispered liaison of the Comtesse Du Barry and the wealthy Duc de Brissac, duly hoped to entice his ladylove to express her admiration for one or two of the exquisite items of great beauty and price which they displayed before her. Then they, in their turn, would lay them before the Duc, who rarely abstained from purchasing the gems for the woman he adored. On one occasion the famous jewellers Boehmer asked to be received in great secrecy by the Comtesse, Madame Du Barry, intrigued, acceded to their request. When they arrived the following morning they again alluded to the necessity for the utmost discretion. The Comtesse assured them that no one would know of their errand. Slowly almost with reverence they produced a velvet sheath and with bated breath they opened it and revealed the most unbelievably beautiful necklace. Jeanne gasped as the room lit up with the brilliance of the diamonds. Then Monsieur Boehmer spoke, 'The stones are unique, it has taken years to collect them, we would like the Queen to own this treasure, we thought that you alone through some channel could arrange that Her Majesty should view them.' Madame Du Barry, still under the impression of this magnificent jewel, thanked them for allowing her to gaze upon such a wonder, and added, 'If I can find a messenger to approach Her Majesty I shall inform you.'

(This was the necklace which caused the famous episode of *Le collier de la Reine*.)

All that day Madame Du Barry carried before her eyes the vision of those diamonds. Then the idea flashed through her mind, could she secure the necklace for the Queen, perhaps this would bring her recognition. By now the wish to be acknowledged by Marie Antoinette had become a mania. Madame Du Barry decided to act and in a moment of folly she told Chon to leave for Versailles, and very discreetly and secretly to persuade her Court friends, who had access to Marie Antoinette, to deliver the following message: 'That should she wish to possess the necklace, Jeanne Du Barry would be honoured if her Majesty allowed her to be instrumental in acquiring it for her. Naturally the transaction would be carried out unknown to a living soul.' Chon returned, she had been able to carry out Jeanne's instructions, so Jeanne waited for a sign from the Queen. It never came. She was told that when Her Majesty received the note she was standing in front of the open fire, she had read it, then without any comment had thrown the message into the flames. Jeanne realized that she had aimed too high and that the Queen of France had contemptuously shown that for her the Du Barry did not exist.

In the vicinity of Louveciennes stood a small château, it had been empty for some years. The peasants in their love for the supernatural had woven a tale concerning its history. They would tell with a look of conviction that they knew it contained an open coffin in which lay a witch. If anyone entered the castle she would rise and stab them, this was why the owner had never returned. One day to their dismay an Englishman, Mr. Henry Seymour, driving past, discovered the small property and took a fancy to it. With his Norman wife, whom he had lately married, he took up residence in this *soi-disant* haunted abode. No ghosts; no coffin, no witch! The people were frustrated and their love of the weird shaken. Quite naturally, Henry Seymour and the Comtesse Du Barry became acquainted. Cordial relations were soon established and invitations exchanged. That is all that was surmised at first, but a far stronger tie underlined this apparent platonic friendship. Only a few letters written by Jeanne give us the clue. The first letter which is undated and bore only the hour when written, contained but a few remarks about neighbouring matters, and regrets to hear that his daughter was ill. She sent a little dog as a present for the child. The second read that she was sending him as a memento a coin of the time of Louis XIV. He had presented her with a small dog in return for the one she had given to his daughter. She mentioned that the puppy was well and could drink by itself. The succeeding letters show that Henry Seymour had declared his passion and evidently had attained his aims. Madame Du Barry writes, 'The assurance of your affection, my tender friend, is the joy of my life. Believe me that my heart finds these two days which separate us long, if it was in my power to abridge them, the pain would cease. I await Saturday with all the impatience of a soul which is entirely yours, and I hope you will not be disappointed. Adieu, I am yours alone.' In these letters the courtesan had ceased to exist, perhaps for the first time in the life of the Comtesse Du Barry, real love had replaced sensuality. She felt a renewed youth in the arms of this man.

What fluctuations of feelings took place between the two lovers! Love, suspicions, recriminations had started, Seymour wanted more, she had to tread cautiously between him and Brissac. She was now thirty-seven, and still divinely lovely, one of the greatest *amoureuses* of her time. The passionate letters continued: 'My heart is entirely yours no one shares it, if I have failed in my promise, my hands alone are responsible. I have ailed since you left me, and I can assure you that I had no strength except to think of you. Come early.'

The Duc de Brissac had become exceedingly jealous. Between the one she was fond of and the other whom for the moment she adored, the Comtesse had to play a difficult game, but in such a situation she was an expert, she had so often faced similar circumstances.

Another letter to Seymour: 'I am so tired I have written four letters. I have only the strength to tell you that I love you.

Tomorrow I shall explain why I was unable to give you news of myself, but believe me that you are the only friend of my heart.'

Things were getting more involved, the suspicions of the two men who now hated each other, were becoming clouds of anxiety for Jeanne. She writes to Seymour: 'I will not go to Paris today as the person I was to meet came here on Tuesday (Brissac) just as you left me, I think you were the subject of this unexpected visit, I was greatly embarrassed. Notwithstanding your injustice I wait for you with all my heart, you know that it can belong only to you. My one regret is being unable to tell you this at every moment of the day.' Evidently Henry Seymour was finding it difficult to face a situation with a wife and mistress living so near one another, so with the excuse of Brissac's interference, he wrote a letter without delicacy or tact. His excuse was that he would not share her body with another man. Jeanne, heartbroken, wrote her last letter.

'It is useless to mention my tenderness and sensibility, you are aware of both, but what you are ignorant of is my misery. You have not deigned to reassure me of what affects my soul, so I suppose my tranquillity and my happiness will not touch you. It is with regret that I mention this, but it is for the last time. My head is well but my heart is suffering, but with much courage and perseverance I shall no doubt succeed in overcoming it. This task will be painful but it is necessary, it is the last sacrifice which I am called to make, my heart has done the rest. It is now left to my reason to do this one.

Adieu, believe me that you alone will occupy my heart.

This Wednesday, midnight.'

After the revolution these letters were discovered in a drawer of a writing-cabinet, which Seymour evidently had left in his home when the Terror broke out and he fled to England.

The Duc de Brissac's devotion saved Jeanne Du Barry. Unselfishly he cherished her at a time when her distracted craze for Henry Seymour was leading her into danger. He took her to visit his numerous properties in Normandy, at first she was not a cheerful companion, but the insouciance of her nature reacted soon. The charm and smiles, which had ever been an enchantment to the Duc de Brissac, returned. He had won her back. Life re-adjusted itself, Louveciennes and 'Prunay' ignored one another. The Duc now lived more or less entirely at Louveciennes. Many of her old enemies were now seeking her friendship, such as Prince and Princesse de Beauvau, cousins of Choiseul, who asked to be received. Madame Vigée-Lebrun arrived to paint her portrait. In her memoirs she recalls the beauty of her sitter, the mischievous slanting eyes, the lovely teeth just perceived when she smiled, that wonderful hair of which no one could ever define the true colour, falling in loose curls around the oval of the face. Dressed in filmy muslin *déshabillés* which she wore even in the coldest weather, only the skin showed slight signs of the passing of the years.

The Baron de Breteuil, Minister of the King's Household, one of those who had disdained Jeanne in her former role now asked her if she would allow him to pay his respects. In the course of conversation which they had, he mentioned that Her Majesty was anxious to purchase the Château de St. Cloud. The Duc d'Orléans owned it, but he refused to sell unless he received an enormous sum. Breteuil who was a devoted admirer of the Queen, suggested that Brissac, a great friend of Madame de Montesson, whom the Duc d'Orléans had lately married morganatically, might influence the lady to persuade the Duc d'Orléans to lower his demand, and so allow the Queen to buy the property. Jeanne wondered if the Queen knew that she was being approached, but unable to bear resentment she managed to obtain St. Cloud for the Queen at a much lower price.

14

The Queen's Necklace

The Queen writes to the Empress Marie-Therese, 'I fear that the King is not as keen to share my bed as he is of hunting.' Although Louis XVI confides to a friend, 'I enjoy the sensation and regret so much time has been lost.' Yet no dauphin seemed to take root.

At last towards the end of April 1778 subdued whisperings started circulating around. 'The Queen must be expecting a child, she is slowing down her activities.' Then on May 5th the Count Mercy sent a special dispatch to the Empress Marie-Therese, 'There is no shadow of doubt, the Queen is pregnant.' On the 4th of August the official announcement was made to the Court. The people's joy was touching, Te Deums were sung in every parish of the Kingdom and all political differences seemed to disappear, 'We shall have a Dauphin!' Only the two royal brothers, the Comte de Provence and the Comte d'Artois joined in the rejoicing with a wry smile. Then began the difficult and important business of choosing the wet nurses who would have the honour of feeding the heir to the throne of France. Several were kept in reserve, in case the chosen one had not the right nipple to suit the royal baby. All possible precautions were being taken.

On the 18th of December the church bells started ringing, letting the people know that the labour pains had begun. The King and the Princes preceded by the Princesse de Lamballe rushed to the Queen's room followed by the Comtesse de Noailles, 'Madame Etiquette', and numerous ladies-in-waiting. Then a mob of Courtiers male and female pushed themselves into this room and sat around the bed according to their rank. For seven hours they remained gazing at the unfortunate woman writhing in pain. In this stifling atmosphere not a window was open. Then a last agonizing scream from the Queen and the birth but – a girl!

Jeanne Du Barry was told the news late that night; was it spite, but she felt gratified that it was not a boy.

Jeanne's great sorrow at having been abandoned by her English lover had long since lost its sting, Brissac was more attentive than ever. Monsieur de Belleval writes, 'It was eight years since I had seen the Comtesse Du Barry when I paid her a visit at Louveciennes a few days ago, I feared the encounter. After so long would I recognize her? When she met me I found her as beautiful as she was in 1769. The only difference was that instead of being received with that wonderful peal of laughter, tears came into her eyes, I reminded her of the past.'

During the month of April a pension which had been granted to Madame Du Barry in 1769, came to an end and the capital returned to the King. His Majesty graciously replaced it by a capital of twelve hundred and fifty thousand livres, it was a great strain on the Treasury. The new Minister, Calonne, was a casual person and a devoted friend of the Comtesse, so he made no objection. Most of the Du Barry's relations, among whom was Jean, had continued to pester Jeanne's existence with demands for money, insisting they had a right to some part of the fund. She in her carefree way satisfied most of these demands. Although her income was very great and the Duc de Brissac gratified her every caprice, she still owed large sums to her creditors, and she had no notion of the value of money.

Marie Antoinette was grateful for the part Madame Du Barry had played in reducing the high price asked for the Château de St. Cloud, and was beginning to lessen her contempt for the former favourite. She told Breteuil that informally she would like to meet her, but it must be done in such a manner that neither side would be embarrassed. The occasion presented itself most favourably – a masked ball at the Opéra was to take place. Madame Du Barry was informed by Breteuil, who now had become an intimate friend and rarely absented himself from Louveciennes, of all the details of the coming meeting.

The Queen's Necklace

That night in one of the large boxes of the Opéra three people sat talking, the Queen, the Duc de Choiseul and the Comtesse Du Barry. In their masks they were supposed to be unknown to one another, but gradually they forgot their assumed personalities and spoke openly to each other. In that frivolous milieu the Queen's prejudice seemed to have evaporated, Choiseul's hatred to have vanished and Jeanne Du Barry marvelled at this transformation. Towards the end of the evening the Queen assured Jeanne of her benevolence and added, 'If ever you require anything address yourself to me.' When looking at the creature he had fought so bitterly Choiseul must have asked himself whether it had been worth while! Now that the mental ache caused by the Queen's scorn had been removed, nothing seemed to mar the Du Barry's paradise.

One morning a message was brought to her, the jeweller Monsieur Boehmer wished to be received in privacy, it was most urgent. He came in, she recalled that she had not seen him since the day he had shown her the fabulous necklace. He looked distraught and begged her help, explaining that he was in an extremely difficult position. Asking for the greatest secrecy, he said the Queen had bought the necklace, the sale had been negotiated by the Cardinal de Rohan. It was to be paid for in three instalments, and now the first instalment was long overdue and nothing was forthcoming. Would the Comtesse help them? Jeanne told him that she had not known that Her Majesty had purchased the jewel, and she greatly regretted but she could not meddle in this matter. Thus the famous trial of *Le collier de la Reine* began. His Eminence the Bishop of Strasburg, Grand Almoner of France, Cardinal de Rohan, had outraged the Empress Marie-Therese by his behaviour when accredited French Envoy to Vienna. He was not an unscrupulous man, but he was an irresponsible character. Although he kept up a certain attitude of religious grandeur, he shocked the respectable Court of Marie-Therese. His fortune was immense and his family, the Rohans, had made history; he felt almost invincible. He loved show and regardless of his high position led a profane, far from edifying existence. At last

Marie-Therese insisted diplomatically on his recall. The Empress informed Marie Antoinette of all this and helped to increase the unaccountable dislike she had already formed against him. Notwithstanding his wealth and position the Cardinal de Rohan felt humiliated at Marie Antoinette's treatment, she never acknowledged his presence. His one wish had been to gain her favour. So when Madame Lamotte-Valois, an adventuress, enticed him with the promise of the Queen's friendship if he could procure the celebrated necklace for her, he lost all sense of proportion, and so was easily duped by this machiavellian deception.

The self-styled Comtesse Lamotte-Valois was a pretty and ambitious woman, of doubtful origin. Her husband the Comte was a willing associate in the furthering of the unscrupulous plans she determined to carry out. Having ascertained all the details concerning the Cardinal de Rohan, and his great wish of being acknowledged by the Queen, by clever intrigue she had managed to make his acquaintance and little by little had become one of the members of his circle. One day she allowed a remark to escape her; and quite casually mentioned Marie Antoinette's name, relating to a conversation she had had with her that afternoon – Madame Lamotte had never spoken to the Queen in her life, and never would. The Cardinal jumped up, 'Do you know the Queen?' he asked. Madame Lamotte smiled an indulgent smile and said, 'Of course! Her Majesty has complete confidence in me.' That was the beginning of the unsavoury story. The confidence of the Queen for her 'great friend' rose and rose in the fanciful mind of the inveterate deceiver. The trust of the Cardinal in her tales became almost ludicrous, she in the meantime extracting sums of money from him in the name of the Queen's charities. Evidently the astute woman realized that the time had come to show something more tangible to keep the credulity of the Cardinal alive. So she told him that she knew that Marie Antoinette longed to possess a famous necklace that the jeweller Boehmer had shown her, but since the cost was too high she did not like to buy it openly. If the Cardinal could procure it for the Queen, Her Majesty would certainly be very grateful. At this point Madame

The Queen's Necklace

Lamotte produced some letters from Marie Antoinette, which in reality were fakes, and had been written by a great expert in imitating other people's handwriting. Yet the one mistake he had made was in signing them 'Marie Antoinette de France'. The Cardinal knew that this was not the manner in which the Queen signed her name, but Madame Lamotte knew no better. When questioned, she superbly replied that the Queen wrote thus to her intimate friends. It was then that Rohan started gathering this enormous sum to pay the jeweller, he pledged his farms, some of his jewels, and valuables. At last the required sum had been raised and was entrusted to Madame Lamotte. Then the outrageous plan was devised. Late one night the Queen would meet the Cardinal in a thicket of Versailles, and he would offer the casket containing the necklace to her, as a token she would return him a letter and a rose. The difficulty for the infamous Lamotte couple lay in finding a woman sufficiently resembling Marie Antoinette, and willing to play the role; it was not easy. At last after much trouble a young prostitute was selected and made to rehearse the part, she knew nothing of what or whom she was to represent. Rohan had been told that not a word would be spoken during the whole scene, the letter would speak for itself, the Queen would be entirely veiled. Rohan, beside himself with the joy and excitement of the forthcoming evening, poured still more gold into the Lamottes' purse. On the given night the Cardinal, trembling with emotion, made his way to the selected spot, and listened. All he could hear was the thumping of his heart, then came the sound of light footsteps, a rustling of leaves and a slight figure in white veiling appeared. Choking with tears of devotion and respect the Cardinal fell on one knee and reverently kissed the hem of the little street-walker's veil. In her fear of making the wrong gestures the girl had dropped the rose and lost the letter. Clutching the casket proffered by the Cardinal, she fled away. No letter, only a crushed rose for Rohan to pick up!

Shortly afterwards it became known to the police that an individual was offering for sale diamonds of great value. The Lamotte couple were busy taking the gems from their settings, trying to get rid of them in this way without being traced. Knowing that it was a dangerous game, Monsieur Lamotte decided to flee to England with the remainder of the necklace and the large sum handed to them by the Cardinal de Rohan, ostensibly in payment of the jewel.

The Queen, completely innocent of this fantastic plot, continued to pay no attention to the Cardinal. At last when the truth was discovered the Queen insisted on a public trial. In the meantime Monsieur Lamotte had escaped to England with the necklace. Marie Antoinette's wish for a public trial was in truth to prove that she had been ignorant of the whole episode, but from this moment her name became anathema to the citizens of France. Insults of every nature coming from all sides were showered on her, the hatred which had lain dormant against her broke out in all its horror. The people accused her of possessing the necklace and inventing the story that the poor Lamotte had stolen it. That the terrible punishment of the unfortunate woman was at her behest, the Austrian creature was made up of hard cruel feelings.

On the 12th of December 1785 Madame Du Barry was called as a witness to the trial, which was taking place at the Bastille. When she was questioned she maintained she had no knowledge of the affair. But three years before, a woman calling herself the Comtesse Lamotte-Valois, had come to see her begging her to present a plea to the King for the restoration of her family's properties. Madame Du Barry said that the woman had fatigued her with her recriminations, and to get rid of her she had accepted the supplicating letter, and placed it on the mantelpiece and later thrown it into the fire.

15

'Etats Généraux

We are now in the year 1786. Marie-Therese had died. The Queen Marie Antoinette had given birth to a Dauphin followed by another son and a daughter; the latter died shortly after birth. The nefarious drama of *Le collier de la Reine* had ended and the Cardinal de Rohan had been declared free from all blame. Madame Lamotte-Valois, the adventuress, had been condemned to be flogged and branded before being imprisoned in the Salpetrière. After a while she managed to escape and join her husband in England. From her safe position abroad she inundated the whole of Europe with abusive and false stories about the Queen, and she also did not spare the Du Barry.

✣   ✣   ✣

During the Summer of 1788 two of Madame Du Barry's familiar friends and protectors of the old days died, the Duc de Richelieu and his nephew the Duc d'Aiguillon. Each in turn was buried in the family vault at the Sorbonne. When the ceremonies were ended and the mourners had left, the Comtesse Du Barry knelt alone on both occasions beside the sepulchre, mourning for the two great gentlemen who each in their way had used their influence and aided her to gain the summit of her career.

In 1789 France awakened never to slumber again. Up to the present the people had expressed their discontent in undertones, but now the scarcity of bread was becoming a menace. The barns were empty and the multitudes were hungry. The grumbling had turned into loud accusations, 'If there is no bread somebody must be consuming the flour. Since none of us has any, then it must be the Court and the nobles who are hoarding the wheat.' Step by step the population was becoming suspicious, and soon suspicion was changed into certainty. A feeling of rebellion against society agitated the whole country, but in reality the hatred centred on Marie Antoinette, the scornful nickname 'Madame deficit' would soon follow her every footstep.

There had been reports of a few outbreaks of violence, of properties being pillaged and landlords maltreated, but now that Calonne had announced the stark truth of the deficit of the Treasury, the whole Kingdom seemed to rise overnight. When the details were known the citizens became fierce, Calonne was forced to resign and Monsieur Necker was named in his place. The days of submission by the masses were over, they shouted their fury and the King's divine rights seemed to have become a mockery. In this turmoil Louis XVI announced the summoning of the Etats Généraux, the assembling of the representatives of the people. Later it became the Assemblée Nationale. Of a sudden the whole scene was altered, the populace from abuse now shouted '*Vive le Roi*' persuaded that now *they* would be the true rulers of France, they were not wrong.

During all these disturbances Madame Du Barry remained at Louveciennes, Madame Vigée-Lebrun was painting what was to be her last portrait. The windows were open, spring was on the way; they talked, Madame Du Barry was reminiscing of the wonders of Louis XV's time, she said:

'Although much licence was allowed the whole atmosphere was decorous, courteous, deferential towards the King; and women, even the lowest, were always treated with a sort of veneration. I can say this from experience.'

In this peaceful abode the only distraction was the Duc de Brissac's return from Paris with the latest news. He was disappointed he had not been named as a member of the Assemblée d'Anjou. He knew his role would have been important, perhaps that was why he had not been chosen. In the tranquillity of those evenings he would admire or criticize the progress made on the portrait; he had commissioned it as a present for himself. Madame Vigée-Lebrun must often have marvelled at the refinement in which the Duc expressed his worship for Jeanne Du Barry. In his devotion there was a deep denial of self, such delicate attentions scarcely sensed, a tenderness not of this world almost tantamount to a religious cult. In trying to comprehend such immense love one wonders if a human being could ever be worthy of such veneration. The Duc realized the dangerous course the events were taking, and he instructed the two women in the roles they would have to play if anything would happen to him. One evening he returned just before the Assemblée was to be opened, he told them the excitement in the capital was frightening. It all seemed quiet and calm on the surface but he felt that if the events went against the deputies, woe to those who stood in their path and opposed them.

On the 20th October of that year Madame Du Barry had a great sorrow – her mother died. She was a rich woman and left her entire revenues to a niece, poor Monsieur Rançon was completely forgotten. To make good Jeanne assured him a pension of 2,000 livres a year. When one remembers the seamstress Anne Becu having to leave her village on account of her misconduct, trudging on her way to the capital, a child hanging on each side of her skirt, and carrying a few pots and pans, then her subsequent life as a cook, and finally in death honoured as the high and mighty Marquise de Montrabé, owner of a large fortune, life seems a game. Jeanne was deeply affected by her mother's demise; it had been her wish to have a funeral of pomp and ceremony but not to attract undue attention it was decided to have a quiet one.

✢   ✢   ✢

It was late, long past the hour of supper, but the two women in Louveciennes were anxiously awaiting the Duc's return, they knew that the Dauphin was dying. For months he had ailed and now the end of his life was speedily approaching. In the morning Madame Du Barry had been among the throngs at Versailles watching the procession to the cathedral to invoke God's blessing on the Assemblée Nationale. That morning before leaving for the ceremony the Queen had been told by the doctors that there was no hope for the child. As they spoke a cry came from the next room, '*Maman, Maman,* I want you,' but the officers on duty announced, 'Her Majesty's coach awaits here.' As she tore herself away the cries continued. Madame de Staël tells us that it was one of the most heart-rending scenes she ever witnessed. 'Attired in a magnificent violet, white and silver gown, her head adorned with ostrich plumes and diamonds, the Queen could scarcely restrain the tears which glistened in her eyes, she held herself erect with difficulty. She seemed to walk and bow unconsciously, her very soul aching for her son in his little bed, too weak to stir, his lips moving only to ask for *Maman.* In her grief she did not seem to notice the grandeur of the proceedings, the whole town was transformed into a bower of flowers, priceless tapestries were displayed from balconies. The crowds were hanging from the chimney-pots to get a glimpse. At ten o'clock the royal cavalcade slowly moved away from the Palace. At one of the windows a small dying child could be seen, he had been tenderly lifted to look upon the imposing sight, but his eyes were closed, he was too tired to look.'

The Duc de Brissac had been told about the tragedy, so Jeanne Du Barry was aware of the torture which Marie Antoinette was suffering. Her heart bled for the Queen.

The whole sight was superb. First came the Royal pages, in vivid liveries, close behind them Falconers with their birds on their wrists, then the chariot bearing the King accompanied by his brothers. The chariot gleamed in the sun as the rays lit up its gold, the horse's plumes waving in the breeze. The King was greeted with rousing cries of '*Vive le Roi*'. Hardly had the cheers subsided than the Queen's chariot accompanied by the Princesses came into view, but it seemed as if the population had lost their voices, not a cry of welcome was raised. The Princesses looked at one another in amazement, Marie Antoinette did not seem to notice this insulting silence, her ears were filled with the cries of '*Maman, Maman!*' Yet she tried to smile.

Every evening when the Duc returned from Versailles, Jeanne's first words were, 'Is the Dauphin still alive?' Every evening for almost a month Madame Du Barry asked the same question. Then on the 3rd of June 1789 Brissac returned from Paris, and in reply to her oft repeated question sadly shook his head. The Dauphin, pride of Louis XVI and Marie Antoinette, was dead, so now the second son Louis Charles de France, born in 1785 became Dauphin. He was a strong child, clever, well able to rule the Kingdom of France, should a throne still exist for him to sit on. With a break in his voice Brissac related to Jeanne the last moments of this heart-rending scene. The Queen had held her dying son in her arms, then the doctors had noticed a strange transfiguration, the child had opened his eyes and smiled looking at his mother; his look had seemed to go through her and beyond on to another world waiting for him. So with this smile on his lips he had passed on.[1]

Jeanne could not sleep that night. Her heart urged her to write to the Queen and express her sorrow, but her head told her she was not pure enough to intrude in such a sacred grief.

[1] This scene truly happened to a child I knew.

16

The Mystery of the Jewel Robbery

The Etats Généraux were beginning to disagree, the nobles, the clergy and the third estate each claimed what they considered to be their rights. Serious disturbances were breaking out in all the different provinces, and soon the third estate had overridden the two privileged classes. On the 20th of June, in the Cour du Jeu de Paume the Assemblée took an oath not to dissolve until the will of the people prevailed and a new constitution was established.

On the 11th of July 1789 the Duc de Brissac arrived at Louveciennes, he looked agitated. Without any preliminary warning he said, 'I have come to say good-bye, events are becoming dangerously alarming, and I am going to my estates in Anjou to see if I can calm the people. You will not hear from me for some time. Do not worry, but think of me, and be careful of yourself.' He was gone before Madame Du Barry could protest.

The news reaching Louveciennes from Paris was ominous, but although only a few miles away Madame Du Barry felt secure.

On the 14th of July the day seemed made for happiness; Louveciennes was at its most beautiful period of the year. Jeanne was posing for her portrait, Madame Vigée-Lebrun was intent on her work when suddenly she dropped her paint-brush; Jeanne leaned forward on her chair and they both listened, the wind distinctly carried the sound of cannons – the Bastille was being taken. At this moment a letter from a person unknown to her was handed to Jeanne. It read:

'Madame la Comtesse,

A few days ago I learned that a pamphlet was being printed concerning you. By bribing a young man of the Press with a small sum of money, I managed to obtain the first pages of this pamphlet, which I am enclosing. The whole thing seems to be a tissue of lies, but it is apparent that the author intends to distribute these leaflets to all members of the Assemblée, with a view to cancelling your income and returning it to the State. In this moment of lunacy such a happening could suffice to drive the populace to commit crimes which are horrifying.

Mr. Dupin
Hôtel Lamoureux, Rue Verte, Paris.'

Although for a time Jeanne felt worried concerning her future, the warning was quickly erased from her mind. She was incapable of concealing her riches or her expensive mode of life, she was open-hearted and trustful. She talked without caution, criticized loudly, and untidily left important documents lying about. Then she received another letter; she never knew who had written it, but it must have come from someone belonging to her staff – was it the humble Desfontaines, who always seemed to watch from a distance?

'Madame la Comtesse,

I humbly beg you to be prudent in all things, you ought not to talk openly, silence is good, and it is absolutely necessary in the present circumstances. All those who surround us have ears which are intent on hearing every sound. Madame la Comtesse has not enough care for the things which belong to her – her money, her letters and her jewels. I beg Madame la Comtesse not only to be beautiful and amiable, but to be strong of character and to be mistress in her own home.'

All these recommendations altered but little Madame Du Barry's incorrigible carelessness.

Madame Vigée-Lebrun was feverishly trying to finish the portrait of Madame Du Barry. The constant rumbling of the guns disturbed her and in her memoirs she writes. 'I was unable to concentrate on the work I was doing at that moment, tracing the graceful waist and hands worthy of a poet's dream.' During this time Madame Vigée-Lebrun had to visit Paris, but she intended to regain Louveciennes in a few days; she found Paris so full of unrest that she decided to leave France altogether. Now Jeanne was alone to study the unfinished picture. It would not be completed until after the Revolution, and was considered by many as the most attractive of all Madame Du Barry's portraits, perhaps because it was the last one before her death. The canvas shows her sitting at the foot of a tree. She is holding an open book on her knees, her dress is green, quite simple, high waisted, giving a foretaste of the coming fashion. A wide ribbon sustains the bosom which one can perceive from the opening of the low *décolleté*, and the sleeves of an embroidered chemisette cover the graceful arms. Her hair is very fair beneath a white veil. Her eyes with slightly closed lids diffuse a gentle mocking gaze, which is full of caress, the mouth is almost smiling, but so tenderly sad it evokes a feeling of melancholy. Although a little less slender, her colouring a shade less vivid than of yore, this woman of forty-six has retained all the charm of youth.

When Madame Vigée-Lebrun left the unfinished portrait, the Duc de Brissac was already being branded by the Revolutionaries as one of the hated nobles. Jeanne Du Barry's name was also being singled out in that defamatory and obscene paper, *Le Petit Journal du Palais Royal*. It read: 'The Comtesse Du Barry, that infamous Messaline, widow of Louis XV, wants to sell a dozen old horses, to buy in exchange a young foal, which the Duc de Beauvau has procured for her.' The anxiety of Madame Du Barry was alleviated when letters began to arrive from de Brissac. He wrote from Anjou, 'I was recognized at Durtal as being the Governor of Paris, and arrested. For a short time it was a question of my being imprisoned or sent direct to Paris. A messenger was dispatched to the capital, and he returned with the order to release me.' The letters continue full of confidence in the future. The Duc was essentially Monarchist, but felt liberty must be allowed in moderation. In another letter from Anjou, dated 29th of August 1789 he writes: 'The post is not frequent enough, I do not hear often enough from you, Madame la Comtesse. *Mon cœur*, I send you all that my soul can hold of love and adoration.'

The Mystery of the Jewel Robbery

The growing demands of the population for drastic reforms continued. The King, restrained by those who surrounded him, refused. Thus provoked, the exasperated populace decided to go to Versailles, from whence in October they forced the Royal Family to leave and take up residence in the Tuileries in Paris.

On October the 5th, unaware of the drama which was being enacted at Versailles, Jeanne Du Barry was writing to the Duc de Brissac. It was late afternoon; the whole house seemed peaceful, the guns were hushed for the moment, the birds were sleeping, the cattle were resting, nothing stirred; she seemed to become part of that calm atmosphere surrounding her. Then from afar a slight noise ruffled that peace, steps were approaching, her trusted man-servant came in and told her that two men in a distressed condition begged to see her. She hurried to meet them; what she saw made her feel faint. Two Swiss Guards with gaping wounds had escaped the onslaught at Versailles; with difficulty and in fear they had dragged themselves to Louveciennes to beg for shelter. Most of their companions had been killed, and their heads carried in procession on spikes behind the King and Queen's coach. They related the terrors of the early part of the day, how a mob of women, of the roughest kind, had marched all night from the capital to Versailles. They had walked in the pouring rain, putting up their skirts over their heads to keep off the torrent of water, by then the crowd had been augmented by men, forming a formidable army. General Lafayette had tried to stop this demented and savage mob from attaining their aim of forcing the King and Queen to return to Paris, but the task had become beyond his control. On reaching Versailles the brutal throng had rushed into the château, slaughtering the King's Swiss Guard. This horror had been perpetrated mostly by a giant of a man, mowing off their heads as he advanced, with an axe. They rushed to the apartment of the Queen, who just saved herself by running into the King's apartment, with only a skirt over her nightgown and without shoes or stockings. In reality the whole attack had been against her; the cries of 'We want bread', and 'The King and Queen to the gallows' had been shouted. Jeanne knew of the risk she was taking in sheltering these men, but without a thought for herself she had a room prepared and food procured, and being sure of the discretion of her doctor she sent for him to tend their wounds. After a few days they got away to safety. The departure of the Royal Family was the end of the glory of Versailles. The reign of the Tuileries started, with all its anxieties and ultimate tragedy; but unlike Versailles, which still stands for the pleasure of the tourists, the Tuileries would disappear, only the trees which still remain remind the world that once a Palace filled with treasure stood there.

The Queen, now more or less a prisoner at the Tuileries, heard of Madame Du Barry's kind act. She asked one of her reliable friends to contact the Comtesse and to express her grateful thanks for the great courage she had displayed in sheltering these wounded young men in her home, thus saving their lives. Still under the stress of that terrible drama the Comtesse asked the Queen's emissary if he advised her to write in answer. He sadly replied, 'Sympathy means much to Her Majesty, the Royal Family's position is constantly menaced. They are separated from all those whom they can trust and surrounded by those whom they cannot trust.' Although she felt unworthy to address the Queen, Jeanne Du Barry asked him to wait while she wrote.

'Madame,

These young wounded boys had only one regret, it was that they did not die with their companions for a Princess so perfect, so worthy of all homage as your Majesty. Louveciennes is yours Madame, is it not? It is through your benevolence and kindness that it was mine again. The late King, who seemed to have been guided by a presentiment, forced me to accept the thousands of precious objects which surround me. I had the honour Madame, to offer you this treasure at the time of unrest, I offer it to your Majesty once again. I beg of you Madame to allow me to render to Caesar the things which are Caesar's.

I am your Majesty's very faithful servant and obedient subject,
                                        Comtesse Du Barry.'

The Mystery of the Jewel Robbery

By now many of the aristocrats were emigrating to different countries, the great centre was Turin. The King and Queen realized the desertion and valued the faithfulness of those who remained. As soon as the Duc de Brissac heard of the danger to the Royal Family he hurried to Paris. On account of his office as Grand Panetier he had to reside at the Tuileries, but it did not prevent him from travelling every evening to Louveciennes to pass an hour or so of enchantment with his adored one. A letter which was discovered long after the author and receiver were no more will give an idea of Brissac's state of mind:

'Madame la Comtesse,

I am going to bed dear heart in hopes of my cold being less violent, and perhaps tomorrow I shall be better company than I would tonight. This cold is caused by the rigours of a long sojourn in Paris. I am unaccustomed to this, and if I have to remain any longer it will either kill me or make me despondent. I hope I will not have to wait too long. I do not want to dwell on this too ardently as the anticipation of the event might retard its realization. Adieu my tender friend, I love you and embrace you a thousand times from the depth of our hearts. I wanted to say, "my heart", but I will not erase what my pen has traced knowing that our hearts are for ever one. Adieu until tomorrow. I am going to try to sweat and spit – a pretty look out! Yet an occupation less disagreeable under the present circumstance than if the weather was calm and consequently fine. All that is passing around us is mysterious and mad. The only sane thing is for us to be together. Adieu tender friend, adieu dear heart, I love you and embrace you.

Brissac.'

The year 1790 was progressing uneventfully at Louveciennes. Madame Du Barry continued her charities, few people came to see her, since travelling had become a doubtful pleasure. More and more aristocrats were leaving France. The Orléans family were spreading damaging tales about the Queen, the Duc d'Orléans and his young sons were attending the assembly of the people, which was becoming all powerful and known as the Assemblée Nationale. Jeanne was more conscious of danger, and did not keep compromising papers, yet she could not keep away from politics and still gave her opinions uselessly. In a very discreet manner she was helping persons whom the Government suspected to flee the country. She had taken two small houses near the coast, smuggling into these houses many who were in peril, and finding means for them to cross the Channel. As yet Jeanne was left completely unmolested.

On the 6th of January 1791, the feast of the Epiphany, the Duc de Brissac gave a fête in his Palace in Paris to celebrate the event, of course Madame Du Barry was present. Afterwards as it was getting late, the Duc asked her to remain and spend the night in his house. Next morning news was brought to her that thieves, aware of her absence, had broken into her room at Louveciennes and got away with the whole of her magnificent jewellery. None of the household had heard a sound. Then details came through. The valet whose duty it was to watch over the treasure, profiting by his mistress's absence had slept out, and the young soldier whose duty it was to watch the property had left his post. The loss was irreparable; much of her capital was tied up in these gems. The Duc was overcome with remorse as his conscience made him aware that had he allowed his beloved to return to her home the night before, the jewels would still be in her possession. Madame Du Barry consulted with her principal jeweller, Rouen, and a list was drawn up of the missing articles. (The list is too long to enumerate here.)

Without reflecting on the dangers which they might arouse, pamphlets describing the stolen jewels were printed in large letters, bearing a final notice of '2,000 livres reward' in still larger letters, and were distributed all over Paris. In reality this brought the Comtesse Du Barry's name before the public and eventually led to her death-warrant.

In the stolen caskets lay the exquisite art of the eighteenth century, the purest diamonds, the most luxurious pearls, the sets of every precious stone. Some of the bracelets displayed the miniature of Louis XV encased in diamonds and of enormous value. The one question on everyone's lips was, how could a few men carry the weight of such a mass of plunder? The pamphlets drew much comment and brought back to the multitude the almost forgotten name of Madame Du Barry, once again the ancient memories were revived. Suddenly the old loathing for the King's mistress became alive, all the legends of her past were passed from mouth to mouth. Even Marat who was becoming the oracle of France wrote an article in the infamous paper *l'Ami du Peuple*. 'The cost of keeping up the Assemblée Nationale during the whole year does not amount to a quarter of what has been stolen from one of the whores of that old sinner Louis XV. See how he enriched that Du Barry, who at one time trotted in the dung of Paris. Oh! if you had seen her twenty years ago covered in diamonds, showing herself off at the Château de Versailles, and giving by handfuls to those robbers, her relations, the golden sovereigns of the nation.' Soon the story was launched that the robbery was a pure invention by Madame Du Barry who feared that her income might be in danger of being reduced, and who imagined that a robbery might dissuade the Assemblée Nationale from confiscating some of her wealth, as they would think her capital had greatly diminished, and was not worth troubling about. In fact it had been severely reduced; much of it lay in those caskets.

17

Visits to London

The Duc de Brissac was determined to retrieve the treasure. He corresponded with different countries and wished to organize a world-wide search for the culprits. Perhaps as a result of this correspondence the facts of the great robbery became known in England. It was curious that in the midst of the search a British agent named Parker Forth appeared at Louveciennes. He was a frequent visitor there and even stayed now and then. The whole business seemed to become very complicated. This man was one of the numerous agents of the British Minister, Pitt, he was redoubtable, clever and ruthless. As far back as 1789 the French Ambassador in London was warning his government to beware of the activities of this man. Why he should have been employed by the Du Barry is inexplicable. It is a matter of surprise that such a notorious detective and well-known spy as Parker Forth was engaged to recover the jewels. The French Government knew all about his reputation and always followed his tracks. Parker Forth became Jeanne's adviser, even during her trial at the end of her life. This association was responsible for one of the charges laid against her. Madame Du Barry did not show undue worry about the loss of her gems; this struck the people as strange. It was true that all over Europe a search was being organized!

At last on February the 14th, a whole month after the theft, Madame Du Barry was told that her jewels had been recovered. Parker Forth had easily detected the culprits – three Germans, a Frenchman, and an Englishman named Harris. Terrified that they might be caught red-handed they determined to rid themselves of the loot, so in their haste they were offering the gems at ridiculous prices. Since almost every country had heard of the robbery, a jeweller named Simon became suspicious, informed the police and the whole plot was exposed and the bandits arrested. Parker Forth let her know that no steps to recover them could be undertaken until she could come to England to identify the jewels. The Duc de Brissac, greatly relieved, organized her journey. It was quite an undertaking in those days and the preparations took some time. Jeanne Du Barry dreaded leaving Brissac; events had seemed to worsen in France. Her great concern was whether she would be allowed to return to Paris. Every day new decrees were proclaimed, but too much was at stake for her to hesitate. So with a large retinue of maids and valets, Brissac's A.D.C., the Chevalier d'Escourre, and her jeweller, Rouen, she sailed for England. On February the 19th she arrived in London. Parker Forth, who had engaged rooms for her and all her companions at the Grenier Hotel, in Jermyn Street, met her on her arrival. The hotel was well known, many of the *émigrés* would stay there on their arrival, until they found accommodation elsewhere. London looked so shabby after the brilliance of Paris, the streets were narrow, especially her street, and the shops dull. She knew only a few of the *émigrés* who were living in that City. Certainly Parker Forth was not the person to introduce her to Society. As she had to sign and attend to numerous business papers and was not sure of how she would be regarded by her fellow countrymen, she remained quietly in her rooms, longing for Brissac and Louveciennes. On the 1st of March she returned to France. Secretly she had been watched and her every movement recorded by an agent of the Revolutionary Government, a man named Blache. He had noted the spy Parker Forth scarcely left her side and that during the last days in London she had met Madame de Calonne, wife of the Prime Minister in Louis XVI's government. The man Blache was to describe these matters more fully during her trial. She was able to see Brissac and rest at Louveciennes for a month. Then a second appeal was sent to her to return to London, as difficulties had arisen concerning her jewels. One wonders if these visits were not for the purpose of secret negotiations concerning the Royalist Party. Once again, accompanied by Parker Forth and her numerous staff, she entered Grenier's Hotel. She was becoming known. The *London Chronicle* announced her arrival – 'The Comtesse Du Barry arrived from Paris yesterday morning. She is staying at Grenier's Hotel. The Comtesse is to attend the Courts concerning her magnificent jewels which are valued at 2,000,000 livres.'

The announcement seemed to attract many of those who had known her in the days of Versailles. She was still beautiful and her renown attracted society, the Prince of Wales wished to make her acquaintance. When she was introduced to him he said after a little while, 'Tell me truly, Madame la Comtesse, what is your impression of London society compared with that of Paris?'

'Monseigneur,' answered Jeanne, 'London is a dignified dowager, Paris a flower girl.'

The Prince was enchanted with her clever remark. She returned to Louveciennes on the 21st of April. Two days later during the night of the 23rd she was awakened and told that she must leave again for England, it was urgent. What did it all mean, did Brissac know? So again she crossed the Channel, this time to remain four months. In reality it all seemed obscure, was she playing a dangerous role aided by Forth? Did she realize that Blache, the French spy, was reporting her every movement?

The newspapers in England announced the Comtesse Du Barry's arrival, English society was astonished and wondered what had hastened her return, the French Royalists seemed to know. Tired of Grenier's Hotel and desirous of greater freedom than an hotel can allow, she rented a large house in Margaret Street, near Oxford Street, which soon became a centre of elegance. She entertained once again, but this time on a much larger scale. Money did not seem to count. It was learned that she had been granted a letter of credit on Simond & Hankey for an unlimited sum from the Paris Banker Vandenyver. That credit was one of the many charges brought against her during her trial. How had she used the fabulous sum? Monsieur Blache and his subordinates were massing endless information for their employers about her. Most of the *émigrés* were now cringing at her

feet and unashamedly swallowing Jeanne's food, she had secured
a chef from France. The Prince of Wales with his lady of the
moment, would invite himself to her parties. By now many of the
most exclusive members of English society were pleased to be included in her receptions. In return she was invited everywhere,
and thus the Comtesse Du Barry shone in the capital of Britain.
Many of the French Royalists would visit her when alone. Some
of the spying servants would report to Monsieur Blache the conversations overheard. So she was watched and the slightest detail
of her daily life travelled back to the Assemblée's secret bureau.
Notwithstanding the remarkable adulation of London society, her
heart felt cold and empty. She knew that her position was unreal,
the only security was at Louveciennes and Brissac, all this buzzing
of individuals around her meant so little. Yet Forth persuaded her
(it was said) to remain until the English Court of Justice had
pronounced its decision on the matter of her jewels. At last it
came; the case must be tried in Paris by French judges; as the
theft had taken place in that country, the judgement must be given
by the French Court. So to Jeanne's great relief on the 25th of
August, still accompanied by Forth, she regained Louveciennes.
That night the Duc de Brissac was able to leave the Tuileries, but
only for a few hours. He told her that events were getting beyond
cure, he warned her of danger. He knew that he was one of the
marked ones, but as long as he was sure of her trust and faith in
him, death did not frighten him. He loved her and would do so
until his heart ceased to beat. So in the middle of the night he left
Jeanne. Only a little time remained before his prediction was
realized.

Although ominous threats were heard on every side Jeanne
received the aristocrats who daily flocked to Louveciennes to hear
the news of their relations and friends whom she had met in
England. The portraits of Louis XVI and the Queen Marie
Antoinette were still hanging on the walls. Forth's mysterious
expeditions continued, supposedly to attend to matters concerning
the coming trial regarding the theft of her jewels. In reality she
was 'a woman of the moment' as one of her admirers had said of

her. Her past did not weigh on her, worries were never too distracting to prevent her serenity. Such a character often develops in persons who have been admired, loved, and adored nearly all their life. The sharp edge of any feeling of bitterness has been effaced, but when a great sorrow does come to them they are often unable to live through it, the past adulation has made them more vulnerable.

The secret watch continued, Blache had followed Jeanne back to France. His task was made easier with the help of Zamor, the young boy from Bengal, whom she had cherished like her own child, and who had now become a revolutionary and one of her worst enemies. Together they were drawing up her dossier with incriminating facts, for the use of the secret division of the revolution.

The King and Queen were now almost house prisoners since their attempted escape and their recapture at Varennes. Brissac was still free and he could at will visit '*Mon coeur*' as he called her. Jeanne's life was becoming calmer, many of those who had come at first for news of their families did not renew their visit, so now she was seeing fewer people. The great moment of her day was when Brissac was able to come to her. She and he clung to each other, his love seemed if possible to grow stronger. Then one evening he told her that the King's Guard had been disbanded owing to the Varennes flight, and the Assemblée had instituted a new Guard in its place, the Garde Constitutionelle. 'The only favour left to Louis XVI had been that he was allowed to name its commander – he had chosen the Duc de Brissac.' Brissac could not refuse but he realized it meant his death knell. As they sat together well into the night, he spoke of his fears and of his dread of leaving her. She tried to comfort him, perhaps if he emigrated . . .? No, he could not show fear and abandon his estates and his peasants, many of whom trusted him, it would be cowardly towards them. As the time came for him to leave her the sun was rising; they took farewell of one another. She pointed to the East, 'This is, *mon très cher ami*, a sign of hope; the sun is bringing light to the world.' Brissac shook his head. 'The sun will set, and the darkness will bring chaos once more; the moon is not able to prevail, she is too pale.'

The Assemblée was ever changing old laws and promulgating new ones, ever arresting and filling the prisons with suspected Royalist partisans. The Royalists were busy inventing ways and means of overthrowing the present régime, but they were mere insects compared to the savage creatures multiplying around.

Suspicion was being aroused by the new Garde Constitutionelle, too many noblemen were joining the regiment, too many titles, too many adherents to the old régime, and the Duc de Brissac at the head seemed a source of danger for the state. The new government was as yet far from feeling secure in its position, the least trifle terrified it. Hence their only hope of survival was the instant crushing of any doubtful incident.

At the *séance* of the 29th of May 1792 the Assemblée was opened with an alarming declaration. Many of the Guards loyal to the Revolution had complained that the regiment was becoming a nest of Royalists. They saw it as their duty to report the same, and they advised the immediate arrest of the Commander, the Duc de Brissac, and the disbanding of the regiment. A decree approving this course of action was signed at one o'clock the following morning. The Duc was to be arrested and to appear before the High Court, sitting now at Orléans. The Duc de Choiseul-Stainville, nephew of the late Prime Minister, happened to hear the proclamation. 'I rushed,' he writes, 'to the Tuileries to inform the King and Queen; they were asleep, but they were roused and hastily they appeared. I told them the distressing news and at once they told me to go to Brissac's room and tell him to escape, he had at least two hours to outwit his enemies. The Duc was in bed, I aroused him and gave him their Majesties' message, but he refused to flee. "No, I cannot do so. A Brissac has never run away." Then he looked at the time, it was nearing five o'clock. I pressed him and begged him to leave the country or at least to hide, but he shook his handsome head and asked for paper and ink. Then quietly and calmly he wrote an endless missive to Madame Du Barry. I incessantly interrupted him, trying to reason with him and pressing him to escape at once but Brissac did not hear, his thoughts were with the woman who held his heart, at last I left.' Brissac wrote and wrote, he heard the soldiers tramp, tramp, coming closer and closer. He called his A.D.C., Monsieur Maussabré, and bade him take his letter to the Comtesse Du Barry. The escort found him and roughly grabbed his arms, the Duc de Brissac shook them off, he stood before them unafraid, handsome and full of dignity, and said, 'It is not necessary to exert yourselves, you will only lose some of the strength you will require to arrest the quantities of innocent people on your list. Tell me where you desire me to go and I will follow,' and so he left the Tuileries for ever.

Louveciennes that night of the 30th of May was sleeping. Only in one room candles were shedding their light, the Comtesse Du Barry lay on her marvellously decorated bed. She could not rest, perhaps the silence of the house affected her, only the unexplained creaking of furniture produced now and again a startling sound. Anxiously her thoughts hovered around the Tuileries, ever culminating in the one she now lived for. As yet she did not know of the drama enacted that morning. She knew that Brissac's name was attracting the dread animosity of the rebels. At last exhausted by her fears, she fell asleep – it was five o'clock in the morning. An hour later came a knock at her door, and to her astonishment, her faithful factotum entered and said, 'I have a message for you, Madame la Comtesse, Monsieur de Maussabré is here and desires to see you.' For a few seconds she felt unable to move; with an effort she opened her eyes, and bade her servant to show Monsieur de Maussabré to her boudoir. Hastily throwing a shawl over her shoulders she stumbled into the room. Her heartbeats seemed to stop, it must mean bad news, at once when she perceived him she knew she had been right. His face was drawn, pale as death, his hand shook, as with a deep bow he handed her the letter from the Duc de Brissac. Then the young man led her to a chair, and left her alone. An hour later he returned, she was still sitting on that chair reading the letter. 'I have read it three times,' she said, 'each time I have suffered more deeply.' Monsieur de Maussabré, unable to give her any hope, returned to Paris in case of fresh developments. Unfortunately this letter was never found, but from what was gathered from different sources it must have contained, apart from his love and devotions, many serious injunctions for her safety, begging her to be prudent, and earnest hopes that one day she, and his daughter the Duchesse de Mortemart, might meet and become friends. Almost crazy with anguish and anxiety she wrote the following letter to Brissac. Evidently it was never sent, since after her death it was found amongst her papers. It discloses the state of her mind.

'This Wednesday 11 o'clock

'I was seized with a mortal fear, Monsieur le Duc, when Monsieur de Maussabré was announced, bringing the heart rending missive. He assured me that you were well and that your clear conscience gave you calmness and peace. But I am far from you, and cannot feel the same. I am ignorant of what you are going to do. I suppose you also do not know? I am sending the Abbé Beliardi to find out what he can. Oh! why am I not with you, I could console you and you would receive the assurance of tender love from a friend. In reality you have nothing to fear if reason and good sense exist in that Assemblée. Adieu, I have no more time, the Abbé is waiting and I want him to leave immediately for Paris. I shall only breathe when I know where you are. I am sure that nothing can be found against you concerning the Garde Constitutionelle, so I have nothing to fear. Your conduct has been exemplary all the time of your stay at the Tuileries, you have done so many acts of patriotism. Adieu, if possible give me news of yourself, and never doubt all I have suffered.'

'Paris, 2nd of June, 1792. 3 o'clock in the morning. 'Madame la Comtesse.

I hasten to send you a letter from Monsieur de Brissac, which will inform you that he arrived at his destination without harm. I would have brought it myself, but I have been charged with several very important missions. As soon as I have accomplished my tasks, I shall start for Louveciennes to inform you of many particulars which it is necessary for you to know. The Duc de Brissac has been taken to the ancient Convent des Minimes, rue Illiers, at Orléans, which is now a prison. Meanwhile allow me, Madame la Comtesse, to beg you to accept my deepest respects.

Your very humble and obedient servant

Maussabré.'

Although the note was short it gave Jeanne instant relief. She wondered why the Duc had not addressed the letter direct to her — then realized he did not wish to compromise her. She knew that he was well, and so far, alive!

Jeanne waited and watched endlessly for any sign of news; in fact her life was at a standstill, sleep evaded her. Although her chef invented dishes to tempt her she left them untasted. She sat day and night staring before her at nothing visible. At last her trusted factotum Morin fetched her doctor. He came; kindly and diplomatically he spoke to her, recalling her back to life, urging her that for the Duc de Brissac's sake she should exert herself and try to intercede to save him. Quietly she revived and agreed that he was right, she would strive to save the Duc. At that moment a letter was handed to her, she recognized the handwriting as she had often seen it in the Duc's possession, it was from the Duchesse de Mortemart, his daughter. As she gazed at it she wondered if it was meant for her or only to be forwarded to the Duc. Carefully she broke the seal and unfolded the paper, at the first lines, her heart ceased beating for a second, then a deep feeling of humility enveloped her. Was she worthy of even touching this missive?

'Will you recognize my writing Madame? Three years have passed since you received my note of sympathy at an anxious moment. Now a much greater tragedy has befallen us; you in your friendship, I in my affection. I have suffered torture for two days. Monsieur de Mortemart and I wanted to leave Spa yesterday, but several important people prevented our departure. The danger for my husband was too great with no possible advantage to my father's safety, but I, could I not be of some use to him? Could I help him in any manner if I risked coming to Paris? Could I see him? For your affection and devotion to my father, the person I love and venerate, you have won my eternal gratitude. Please believe in this sentiment which I have vowed to the end of my life.

5th of June, 1792.'

18

The Storm Grows

During the drive to Orléans the Duc de Brissac's whole soul was with Jeanne. He feared that she, ever impulsive, might compromise herself for his sake. The other arrested men were in great distress and kept complaining, he did not even hear their complaints. Many of them asked for his opinion; he had none to give and never answered, his thoughts were far away at Louveciennes, consoling in imagination the one creature whom he yearned for. The convoy arrived at its destination, the Convent des Minimes. The sun had set some time before, and dusk was turning rapidly into night. They alighted; they were almost unable to walk, cramped by the intolerable lack of space. As Brissac stumbled into the sombre entrance a man came up to him, at first the Duc did not recognize him, the lantern hanging from the ceiling gave little light. Then this man said, 'Monsieur le Duc, I heard you were to become one of us living here, I have taken the liberty of vacating my cell number 8 and want to give it up to you.' To Brissac's joy it proved to be Monsieur de Lessart, a great friend and ex-Minister of Foreign Affairs, who had been a member of the lately formed Garde Constitutionelle, which the Duc had commanded. As the Duc protested, this kind person insisted and begged him not to refuse. 'It is more healthy, cleaner and if there is any sun a ray comes through a tiny skylight. After all I have been here for some time, and am almost accustomed to the roughness and the rules of the place. For you, straight from the luxury of the Tuileries, it would be unbearable. Although it is unsavoury and bare, the walls are less dilapidated than the others. Please deign to accept my offer.'

One servant was allowed to attend the Duc. Until certain formalities had taken place the prisoners were kept behind bars. On the 14th of June 1792 the High Court gave an order that the accused might be allowed visits from a few people. Only those with permits would be admitted into the prison, they would be escorted to the prisoners they wished to visit and after a short time re-escorted out of the building. From that time, every day Jeanne sent her old coachman Auguste, and other messengers to Orléans, to take a letter to her lover. As often as possible she would travel with them, but Brissac, anxious for her safety, begged her not to attract too much attention. It must have been during one of these interviews that, unaware of the future, Brissac said farewell to the light of his life.

Madame Du Barry felt calmer, the Duc was tranquil, he knew that nothing could be discovered against his honour. Later she remembered that at that last parting they had spoken only of the future, when once again they would be near one another and how with the passing years their love would grow deeper and deeper and it would finally absorb them until together they would lie in the same grave. She recalled his last words as he had pressed her to his heart, '*Que Dieu nous entende.*'

She wrote to his daughter telling how quiet and sanguine her father was towards all eventualities, and how his sordid surroundings apparently did not affect his daily life. He was above it all, his high mental attributes shielded him from these miserable pinpricks. Jeanne received the following letter in answer to her own, from Madame de Mortemart:

'Spa, 25th of June, 1792.
'I render you a million thanks, Madame, for the news you have the extreme kindness to give me. I have received a missive in my father's own hand, he tells me he is as well as is possible in a prison, and has been interrogated. Notwithstanding his perfect innocence and honesty, I fear the whole procedure will take a long time. For a few days we have been worried by the news

from Paris. The Duke of Brunswick is expected at Coblentz, as well as funds, and both with the same impatience. I feel I had better continue my cure, the waters are horrible and give fever and the mange, but I am assured it is all for the good. Adieu Madame, receive my assurance of my sincere attachment for life.'

✢   ✢   ✢

The Assemblée Nationale was becoming deeply conscious that ruling a nation was a complicated task. They had proclaimed the dissolution of the Garde Constitutionelle, and most of its members had been arrested, they were becoming suspicious of everybody and everything. In the meantime the *émigrés* headed by Louis XVI's two brothers the Comte de Provence and the Comte d'Artois, were agitating and organizing a war against the French Revolution. They had established their headquarters at Coblentz, and were inviting Austria to join them. In the beginning of the unrest Queen Marie Antoinette had written to her brother, the Emperor Joseph II (who had since died) seeking his intervention as the revolutionaries were becoming a danger, but now she realized that in either case there was little hope for her and her husband. If there was an armed intervention by the *émigrés* and France was victorious and the new Emperor of Austria and the King of Prussia had supported it, it was certain that the revolutionaries would no longer permit a King to rule them. If on the contrary France's National troops were defeated by the Royalists it was certain that the infuriated mob would not hesitate to implicate the King and Queen and demand their lives. Seeing the agony of the future, Marie Antoinette wrote to Leopold II, now Emperor of Austria, imploring him to act very cautiously and restrain the over enthusiastic partisans. Leopold II realized the cause for alarm and in reality personally opposed to war, discouraged the Princes and other refugees and exhorted them to avoid any action which might be ill-construed. Unfortunately Leopold II died in the early part of spring, 1792. Her nephew Francis II, son and heir to Leopold II, scarcely knew his aunt and uncle, the French Sovereigns, but saw his advantage in attacking France and defeating the Revolution. Antagonisms between them flared up and Louis XVI, who had been forced into acknowledging the Assemblée Nationale, was now obliged (it is said, with tears) to declare war on Austria; this was on the 20th of April 1792.

From this moment the King and Queen were doomed. Immediately an *émigré* army on foreign soil came into existence, an army organized, an army fighting for a purpose. The French revolutionary forces, though untrained, were ready to oppose and repulse an enemy who evidently intended to restore the régime which they had displaced, but each man decided to act as he thought best since he was now a free individual and owed obedience to no one.

Events were alarming, the population were openly blaming the King, and the word 'traitor' was being murmured on all sides. The Duke of Brunswick commanding the Allied army was nearing the frontier of France. In his imprisonment the Duc de Brissac heard indirectly of King Louis XVI, Marie Antoinette and their children's internment in the Temple. His heart sank at the prospect of Jeanne being molested whilst he was not near to protect her. That same evening he realized that perhaps his turn would come next and he must put things in order as far as he could at present. He had been hesitating about making a will; the thought that perhaps soon he might be free, and able to do it officially, had deterred him. Now he could only make it out in the form of a letter to his daughter expressing his last wishes. Late that night his cell was already dark, the oil in the lantern was low, he felt that like the oil he had little time before him. He sat down on the wooden stool, drew the lantern towards him and wrote. He appointed his daughter the Duchesse de Mortemart sole legatee, and after having expressed his wishes as the head of the family he added a codicil. 'I recommend ardently to my daughter a person who is dear to me and whom the present difficult times may place in great distress. My daughter will receive a private codicil which will explain my orders on the subject.' The codicil read: 'I grant to the Comtesse Du Barry de

Louveciennes, over and above my gifts to her a net income of 24,000 livres.'

The oil was still giving a dim light, he hastily wrote to Jeanne,

'This Saturday, 11th August, 1792.

'This morning I received the most delightful of letters, one which pleased my heart. I thank you, I embrace you a thousand thousand times. Yes, you will be my last thought. We know of no details. I moan, I shiver. Ah! dear heart why cannot I be in a desert with you, instead of at Orléans, where it is far from agreeable. I embrace you thousands and thousands of times. Adieu dear heart. The town is quiet so far.'

Suddenly Madame Du Barry's name seemed to blaze into prominence. Until the present time she had resided in her house without being disturbed. But the Assemblée, ever on the warpath, rejoiced to find a new victim to terrorize. On the 19th of August 1792 a perquisition was carried out at Louveciennes by the Garde Nationale. Monsieur de Maussabré, who was being hunted down on account of his connection with the Duc de Brissac, had sought refuge with Jeanne. When the Guards made their order known, she hastily hid the young man behind a bed, and boldly told the soldiers that she was alone in the house with her servants. They rudely pushed her aside, and with their bayonets attacked the furniture and every corner of the house, ruining valuable materials, and breaking irreplaceable china. At last they found their quarry, Jeanne begged them to leave him with her, as he was ill with fever and could barely raise himself. Most of them were drunk, and they kept reeling around the beautiful rooms which they had ransacked, spitting on the priceless carpets, and shamelessly relieving themselves in corners. One egged the other on, stupidly laughing and mocking her supplications. Jeanne realized she could do nothing. Dragging the fever ridden Monsieur de Maussabré, they shook, punched and kicked him atrociously. On the threshold of the house he turned his eyes towards her and said, 'Thank you Madame for all you have done, God bless you.' Later she learned that he had been taken to the Abbaye de Saint-Germain, where he suffered a terrible death during the September massacres. To escape the assassins storming the prison, he had climbed up a chimney. They had set fire to it; suffocating in the smoke, he had fallen down, upon which the brutal horde had shot him.

19

Massacre

Louveciennes was unrecognizable, all its luminosity had fled, only dread had replaced its radiance. On the 2nd of September 1792 the faithful Monsieur d'Escourre came to Louveciennes. It was nearly two o'clock in the night. All was dark, but from Madame Du Barry's bedroom a dim light could still be discerned. He knocked softly, hoping that he might be heard. His news was important, and he wished to inform her quietly and not rouse the household. She had heard the knocking and opened the door, stealthily they mounted the stairs and entered her boudoir. She seemed shattered with terror, realizing that this nocturnal visit meant danger. Monsieur d'Escourre related to her that a few hours ago he had learnt that the Assemblée had decreed that the Garde Nationale at Orléans should be recalled to Paris, and that the prisoners should be transported to the Château de Saumur, near the city. To protect the prisoners, they would send eighteen hundred soldiers to escort them, commanded by Fournier, an American adventurer. Jeanne had heard of this ferocious individual, she shuddered, she was too horrified to articulate. Monsieur d'Escourre left her at dawn; he thought it was safer to regain Paris and to discover what was taking place. She, poor woman, remained in a state of stupor. When Mlle. Roussel came in to draw the curtains, she had a shock; Jeanne lay on the floor, her eyes wide open, in her terrible anxiety she must have slipped from the sofa, and in her unconsciousness had remained where she fell.

Jeanne let a few days pass, then unable to bear it any longer she resolved to leave for Paris, to try and unravel the truth. In the midst of her preparations Monsieur d'Escourre sent her a message, telling her that on no account must she come to the capital; she was suspected and the least seen of her the better for her, he would visit her shortly. The truth was that he knew the worst and did not dare inform her. On the 3rd of September the ignoble Commander Fournier had allowed his men to pillage the prisoners of all their belongings; even the few pictures of those they loved had been looted, sacred ornaments had been broken and trampled upon. They were helpless, Fournier had watched the scene with a devilish smile of contentment. Then the fifty-three prisoners had been told to follow the soldiers. As they emerged into the yard they had been piled into carts which awaited them, and told to sit in the straw which smelled strongly of cow dung. Dazed they had squeezed against one another, they had been told nothing, they possessed nothing. The soldiers had kept snarling at them whilst holding up somebody's treasured possession. The convoy started, as soon as they came into the road they had been met by shouts and cries of 'Down with the conspirators, down with the traitors.' They were badly shaken in these vehicles, and so many people in a small space was almost unbearable. The only food they had been given was bread and water, and not much of that. At last they had reached Etampes, where they had halted for a day, still huddled in their carts, but able to rest from the terrible swaying. Although the order of the Assemblée had been that the prisoners should lodge at Saumur, for their safety, Fournier, who was in command, had decided to take them straight to Paris. As they neared Versailles, the howls of the mob became fiercer. The tumult increased and like one voice the cry for vengeance went forth. 'Death to the high and mighty noblemen.' The Duc de Brissac who was standing up was recognized, now the whole tone became more personal. 'Give us at least Brissac, we want a victim.' The Duc did not show a tremor of fear, notwithstanding his undignified position he still looked outstandingly handsome in his blue and gold trimmed habit, his high boots, his hair rolled into tight curls. An old market woman who had yelled herself hoarse suddenly changed her tune and shouted, '*Mais t'es ben beau, t'es ben trop beau pour mourir!*' The Conseil de la Commune, alarmed at this demonstration of vicious fury by the mob, declared that to safeguard the prisoners they should be confined to the cages which used to house the animals of the zoo at Versailles, but the possibility of reaching the place seemed remote. The order was given to change the route so as to avoid passing through the town, the convoy was driven in a zigzag manner by highways and byways in the hope of avoiding the bloodthirsty crowd. The noise, the obscene words, the threats, the clamour came to the prisoners from the adjoining streets. The terrifying fiends seemed to have cut off all retreat. As the convoy neared the Orangerie the guards rushed forward to push open the gates, but they were locked. Now the mob had obtained arms – swords, knives and pickaxes. The guards who were supposed to protect the prisoners were dispersed, and were not showing much enthusiasm to save their charges. The insults were directed mostly against the Duc de Brissac and Monsieur de Lessart, his kind friend. Amid the deafening noise, one could plainly discern the sinister words 'We want their heads.' The throng threw their weight against the carts, they ruthlessly assailed the third vehicle in which stood the Duc de Brissac and Monsieur de Lessart. It overturned; the other occupants scrambled out, but the Duc de Brissac and Monsieur de Lessart, who tried bravely to defend themselves with their bare hands, were struck over and over again amidst ferocious howls of triumph. Then they were set upon with knives and bayonets, and were literally torn to pieces. A last blow cut off the head of Brissac, and that beautiful head was stuck on a pitchfork! The man who had done the deed was covered with blood, and sang victoriously. A raucous voice rising from this dementia shouted. 'Let us go to Louveciennes,' immediately a procession started engulfing the whole crowd. A deathly hush fell upon the scene of carnage, fifty-three bodies lay strewn on the blood-soddened earth, one head was missing, it was on its way to Louveciennes!

On that day the 7th of September, Jeanne Du Barry was alone at Louveciennes, only her maid the faithful Mlle. Roussel had remained. All the other servants had gone to Paris in the hope of gathering some information concerning the Duc. The house was very still, Jeanne could almost hear her heart beating, how long the day seemed, waiting for the return of her servants. Then

Mlle. Roussel burst into the room, exclaiming that there was a rumour in the village that the prisoners of Orléans had been released and that Monsieur le Duc might come to Louveciennes that evening. If he did, continued Mlle. Roussel, the villagers had decided to greet him and escort him here. So in anticipation of the possible event Jeanne decided to wear his favourite gown, the white satin one with the blue sash and muslin fichu fastened by a rose, around her neck a diamond chain with a medallion encasing a miniature of her beloved. Still the house was noiseless – none of her staff had yet returned – only her maid, Mlle. Roussel, had come back from the village. 'How lovely you are Madame la Comtesse,' she said. 'Monsieur le Duc will be happy to see you again. The rumours are persistent that he will be here before night-fall, and many of the villagers will be happy to see him back.' Then from the far distance came a distinct reverberating sound, Jeanne quickly rose from her chair and opened the large windows. Ah! could it be him being escorted back by those village people Mlle. Roussel had told her about? She heard cries, then shouts, oh yes! it must be the Duc. The tramping of feet became more audible, she could scarcely breathe, then Mlle. Roussel rushed in, 'Does Madame la Comtesse hear, it must be Monsieur le Duc being welcomed home!' the noise was getting louder, the *curé*'s old cook passed by, she was running home. '*J'ai peur*,' she called out. Jeanne was trembling, the procession was almost at the gates; it entered, she stood holding on to Mlle. Roussel, she heard, 'Brissac is coming back to his whore, let them enjoy each other.' She saw something wobbly carried like a bundle on a pitchfork. Part of the procession had followed the ghastly sight, others had re-mained outside the gates. Almost unconscious Jeanne stood staring, yet she could not distinguish what was the object they were holding up. The man who was bearing it approached the window and amid wild applause he hurled it into the room. It rolled towards Jeanne; as she retreated a few steps it landed at her feet. In horror she looked down, then she recognized the Duc's eyes, they were open and seemed to ask for her pity. The face was no longer human, the flesh was hideously lacerated, for a few moments she turned into stone, she felt nothing, she said nothing. Mlle. Roussel led her tenderly away from the revolting scene. Then the mob's hatred turned to the garden, the beautifully tended flower beds were crushed and trampled upon, shrubs were torn asunder, the trees hacked to pieces, until finally exhausted by their wanton behaviour, the distorted faces and hoarse voices passed on their way to the capital to seek more victims. Much later when night had fallen Mlle. Roussel re-entered the room and by the light of a dim candle she reverently carried the remains of that once handsome head and buried it in the garden. Many years later a gardener came across a skull at Louveciennes, it must have been the skull of the Duc de Brissac. So his last desire had been fulfilled, he had lain at the feet of the woman he had worshipped! The next morning when Jeanne's cup of chocolate was brought up to her, the bedroom was deserted, the candles had melted in their sockets long ago, the fire was out, the bed unslept in. Jeanne had requested to be left alone. They found her in her boudoir sitting in the same armchair in which they had left her the previous evening. A few days later she wrote to a friend:

'I am suffering in body and soul as you can conceive. So the terrifying crime has been accomplished and I am still alive. Sorrow does not kill, but destroys part of one's heart.'

Then in her extreme anguish she wrote to a woman who was in utter desolation, the Duc's daughter, the Duchesse de Mortemart – far away in exile. The Duchesse worshipped her father, and it was said that the grief she experienced never lessened.

'No one Madame, could have shared in your loss more deeply than myself. His destiny which ought to have been so great, so glorious, has ended in horror. Your unhappy father's last wish, Madame, was that I should love you as a sister. This wish is too near my heart that it should not be accomplished. Although I am unworthy of this, perhaps with your beloved father's blessing you will allow it to come true.'

Madame de Mortemart answered:

'This morning, Madame, I received your letter of the 22nd of September. I must thank you for the good it did me, it diminished a little the tight feeling in my heart by allowing me to shed some tears. At least twenty times I took up my pen to tell that my heart is torn, to talk to you of my immense grief, that since I left Paris and my father I have never ceased to crave for him. I hesitated to send you my feelings of the moment for fear of augmenting your distress. The last wish of the one I love and will ever regret is the same as mine. My affection for you is that of a sister, and it will last until my death. I should like to be able to adhere to all the wishes of my father's last moments. I shall not rest until the last one of them has been fulfilled.'

Although Jeanne Du Barry was like a broken reed, and her gnawing grief never relaxed, on the 14th of October 1792 she left once again for England, with her jewels as the usual excuse. In her urge to get away from that ever vivid morbid scene, and with several other unknown motives, Jeanne left alone for London. The question of her jewels seemed almost futile. It was a year since the accused men had been released; the verdict had been 'No sure proof of their having taken the fabulous fortune.' Why did she not insist on gaining possession of them, as they had been found and declared her property? The whole affair seemed uncanny. It was a dangerous moment to leave the country. It is true that she had taken every possible precaution to be allowed to return. Monsieur Lebrun, the Minister of Foreign Affairs, rather influenced by her charm, granted her a passport for six weeks. Later he was severely blamed by the Convention, which had now replaced the Assemblée Nationale, for contemptible weakness.

Jeanne encountered at the port the Duchesse de Brancas, and the Duchesse d'Aiguillon who were emigrating. The latter, fearing to be recognized, passed as Jeanne Du Barry's maid.

20

Regicide

Madame Du Barry was once again in London far away from the barbarous scene in her drawing-room at Louveciennes. Before we follow her last visit to this country let us pause for a few moments and try to analyse the intricate nature of this renowned woman. After studying the different epochs of her life one still has moments of unexpected surprise. It has been said that she was a 'bad woman', that she was prodigiously generous when she thought it would benefit her reputation. Among the tangle of opinions expressed by people who only repeat others, it is perplexing to judge her. But living as it were for over a year with her memory and following as far as possible all the circumstances of her existence and the events which created them, one can only say that Jeanne Du Barry was 'good'. She might have retaliated towards many who made her suffer, yet she used her influence at the time of her power only to beg the King's leniency. Only once did she use the influence of her position, in the case of the Duc de Choiseul, and even then she was reluctant to act. Was it inertia or genuine kindness? Money did not exist for her, she rarely inquired into the question of cost. If she wanted something, that was all! In reality there is only one conclusion – she was 'Grand'. In her youth she walked the streets of Paris, in her mature age she walked the halls of Versailles, always unconstrained, always true to herself. Certain things hurt her, Marie Antoinette's disdain was the principal, and yet she longed to be of use to her on many occasions. Shall we say that although her soul had been soiled by petty and momentous adventures these had certainly not left any permanent mark.

·   ·   ·   ·

Regicide

London in that month of October 1792 was overflowing with *émigrés* most of them in great misery, some literally hungry. When they heard that the Comtesse had once again arrived, they flocked to greet her. She had rented a large house in Bruton Street, near Berkeley Square. Soon it was filled with famished nobles of France. She had large sums at her disposal from her bank. Again comes the question, why all this money? But secretly she was helping people, especially the bishops and priests – their poverty was alarming. She knew of the danger she incurred, but undaunted she continued. Her *salon* was soon invaded by all the celebrated Royalists, it was becoming a centre of political intrigue, the Convention was openly insulted and criticized and the Monarchy glorified. Madame Du Barry, heedless of the future, and still under the bitter sting of the brutal death of her lover, did not subdue the challenge that was issuing from her house. Blache with almost invisible spies was lengthening his list of indictments against her; later they would be produced at her famous trial. English society once again graced her evening receptions, Lord Queensberry accompanied her on her visit to the King. William Pitt, the Prime Minister and greatest enemy of France saw much of her, Lord Hawkesbury and in fact the most renowned members of the British aristocracy were her guests, her success was astounding. A contemporary of that epoch wrote: 'The Comtesse Du Barry received the other evening in her large house, I found myself amongst one hundred and fifty people most of them French, I noted them by their excited voices and fantastic gesticulations. The contrast with the English guests with their low voices, stiff movements and conventional expressions was very striking. The Comtesse is forty-seven years old, I wish I had known her at twenty-seven, but certainly the years have passed her by, she is still very lovely.' The six weeks allowed on her passport had long since elapsed, it had been a case of 'Tomorrow and tomorrow, and tomorrow.' Although Jeanne seemed outwardly to be in a whirl of agitation, in reality her very soul was calm in its sorrow, the glamour, the scenes, the noise around her scarcely reached her soul. In her mind there seemed to exist a task which she must accomplish as an atonement.

✤   ✤   ✤

The news which was allowed to filter through from France was terrifying. The King and Queen were in the greatest peril, and the whole of that beautiful country was in the power of madmen. The terror was overwhelming and people were dying from fear even before being arrested. The excited voices and gesticulations had moderated in Jeanne's *salon*, the future made them tremble – but still they believed the revolutionaries would never dare to touch the King.

On the 21st January 1793 in Paris one of the greatest tragedies occurred. Louis XVI, King of France, condemned by the blood-thirsty Convention was forced up the dreaded steps of the guillotine, and publicly executed!

When the news reached the *émigrés* in London, a cry of horror went forth, 'Sacrilege has been committed!' The whole English population was shocked, at once in all the theatres performances were interrupted and the entire audience and actors sang the National Anthem. In all the Embassies, chapels, and Catholic churches services were celebrated. That night at Madame Du Barry's the *émigrés* came in deep black, some were in old worn-out gowns, as they could not afford new ones. They sat quite silently, tears flowing down their cheeks, saying their rosaries and murmuring prayers. Madame Du Barry in a long black crêpe veil and sweeping skirt assisted at the official service at the French Embassy for the soul of the martyr King.

The whole of Europe was in a state of effervescence. The regicide of Louis XVI had shaken the foundation of Monarchy, of reason, and of power. On the 1st of February 1793 France declared war on England, and William Pitt formed the first Coalition against her. The Comtesse Du Barry continued to render important services to the Royalist cause, thanks to the vast sums of money she had at her disposal. It is known that in January 1793, she provided from London, a sum of two hundred thousand livres to the Duc de Rohan-Chabot, it was paid to the Duc in Paris by the bankers Vandenyver. Evidently it was in aid of the insurrection which had started in the Western provinces of France, and in which Rohan-Chabot seemed involved. The few details concerning the Queen that filtered through were horrifying. Jeanne wondered if, once back in France, she could help her in some way. A curious indecision seemed to retain her in England, yet for certain unknown reasons, to which she alone held the key, she knew she must return. Her indecision was ended when a message reached her that Louveciennes had been put under seal, and her only hope to save the property was to return to France at once. When she announced her departure, there was general consternation. The French *émigrés* and their English friends tried to deter her, but she would not bow to their arguments. The day before she left, William Pitt asked to be received by her. When the Prime Minister entered the room he stood silent for a few seconds; Jeanne looked beautiful in deep mourning, a lovely diamond necklace gleamed around her throat relieving the gloom of her gown. Gazing at her, a feeling of pity overtook him and taking her hand he raised it to his lips. 'Madame, you cannot go back to your country. I have just had startling news. No one will be spared, no one will be safe. Remain here in peace and security.' Jeanne beckoned him to sit next to her and with pleading eyes answered, 'Mr. Pitt do not ask me an impossible thing, my duty calls me back and I cannot disobey its summons,' so he left. A few minutes later, with a smile she entered her drawing-room. It was to be her last reception, the next day she would leave. The reception-room was crowded, most of the gathering had tears in their eyes as they took their leave. They said, '*A bientôt*', she knew it was 'Adieu'.

On the 5th of March, the Comtesse Du Barry left England. Her passport was long outdated. On her arrival at Calais she was informed she could not travel farther until she had her papers reviewed. She sent them to Paris at once. At the same time she was told that Louveciennes was still under seal and that sentinels kept watch. In her letter to the Convention Jeanne had expressed in strong terms her extreme astonishment at being treated like an *émigrée* considering they knew she had gone to London on account of the endless business concerning her jewels. On the 17th of March, her passport was returned to her and permission to regain her property was granted, on the 27th she reached Louveciennes; Mlle. Roussel, Morin and the librarian Desfontaines welcomed her at the gates. As she entered her château a sensation of utter desolation enveloped her – the emptiness, the solitude which seemed to permeate the whole structure, the remembrance of the man she had loved, now there was no one left in whom to confide. How she longed for Chon's sympathy, but she had long ago left for Toulouse. She was startled out of her reverie by crude voices chanting their disapproval. 'She has returned, the concubine of Monarchy!' Morin informed her that many of the villagers had missed her generosity, yet now they were being influenced by a strange man who had taken a room above the public house, and was organizing a campaign against her. His name was Greive, half English, half American and a citizen of the latter country. He claimed to have rendered great services to Washington and Franklin, and admitted being a fanatic revolutionary and friend of Marat. Intoxicated by his self-made importance, why did he select Jeanne Du Barry as a special victim? Was it because Louveciennes stood out as the epitome of luxury, a rendezvous for the few Royalists of prominence left in the Capital? But above all Jeanne was now a defenceless woman and an easy prey. Greive's method of converting the villagers must have been irresistible, in a few weeks he managed to turn the apathetic inhabitants into raging *sans-culottes*, Mister Greive was a hero amongst them. Jeanne was loth to listen to the advice of her factotum, who told her to leave immediately. She had a mission to accomplish before she could take flight, but her wish was to return to England, not to save herself, but to obey that ever mysterious duty. A little later she tried every possible means to secure a passport and permission to travel, but her credit had run out and her request was irrevocably refused.

The Duc de Rohan-Chabot, evidently an active member of the scheme was often at Louveciennes. He was extremely handsome, courageous, dignified and above all a great lover. In her anxious perplexity Jeanne came to him for advice and consolation. Although still in deep mourning for her devoted lover, the Duc de Brissac, she was faltering under the new attraction. The Duc de Rohan-Chabot was free, his wife had died some years ago. He had possessed many women and ruined many homes, but such was life in those days, Jeanne on her side had led a voluptuous existence, it had been her trade. They were no longer in the bloom of youth but the magnet of desire was still charged, and once again, but for the last time, Jeanne Du Barry owned a man's heart as well as his entire being. His love for her was different from Brissac's. Rohan-Chabot demanded all, Brissac gave all. Very little is known of this last liaison. This letter was found among her papers after her death.

'Come to me dear love, and pass the day here. Grant me a few moments of happiness, there are none without you. Come and believe in one who loves you beyond all, above all until the last seconds of his life. I kiss a million times the most enchanting woman that the world contains and whose heart, so noble and so good, merits an eternal attachment.'

This letter was not signed but comparing the handwriting with other minor notes from him, there is no doubt as to the sender. Jeanne had not had the time to burn it.

The Coalition Armies were advancing and the Republicans had just sustained a defeat. The Convention was alarmed and tightened up the laws relating to the nobles still in France. Greive saw his opportunity, he approached the Commissioner dealing with the question and sent a long report signed by thirty-six inhabitants of the village.

'26th of June, 1793.

My duty commands me to awake the attention of the paternal administration to the peril in which our country is, in allowing Madame Du Barry to be a danger to France by her unscrupulous behaviour.' Blache wrote on his side, 'The house of that woman is a refuge for all the scoundrels who conspire against our beloved country.' Then appeared the names of the Royalists who frequented Louveciennes; three of Jeanne's servants were also implicated. The same evening without previous notice Jeanne and her servants were pushed into a carriage and transported to the prison of Versailles. Yet a little later she was taken to the château, did she remember the last time she slept there? She was under the strict surveillance of sentinels, for whom she had to pay. Several of her friends wrote and offered to keep her company during her detention, but Jeanne was determined to regain her liberty, she wrote to all those in authority declaring her astonishment at being arrested. In fact on all sides people were intervening to obtain her release. A petition was sent to the Comité de Sûreté Générale, signed by sixty loyal inhabitants of Louveciennes, describing the amount of good she had done to the villagers, her generosity and her devotion to the sick and the poor. In reality the authorities were not very interested in her case and on the 13th of August 1793, she and her servants were released.

On the 17th of September 1793 a new law was promulgated. It was against those who had shown by their conduct, their discourses, their writings and their connections to be in favour of the tyrants, and against the people's liberty. It was left to the decision of the local members of the Sûreté Générale to make out lists of suspects and to arrest them. The Comité de Sûreté Générale had reorganized itself and its new police inquisition was limitless. Greive, now all powerful, was intent on pursuing his prey unto death. He wrote a long detailed document, which was laid before the Convention:

'Faithful to our principles of devotion to our dear liberty, that creates the happiness of the world, we declare that we intend to arrest a woman too celebrated for her liaisons in the era of the Monarchy, by her vast fortune, and her caresses learnt at the Court of a feeble and corrupt tyrant, and who has so far escaped the punishment due to her. It was from her house that Brissac began his schemes in favour of the Royalist tyrant and against the liberty of the people. It is in her house that every plot against our beloved liberty has been planned. It is she, whose luxury is worthy of a former mistress of a Monarch, who mocks at the sufferings of those who are shedding their blood in our glorious Armies, for liberty.' He ended his declaration with the blood-curdling invocation 'Death to the courtesan of Louveciennes, the bacchante crowned with laurels and roses.' Thuriot, the President of the Convention declared, 'The facts with which you have charged this woman are very grave, you can be assured that if they are proved, her head will fall under the guillotine.'

Now fear, dread, almost panic penetrated the very walls of Louveciennes, and Jeanne Du Barry was unable to surmount the gloom and anxiety it generated. Greive frustrated in his wish for the extermination of the still well loved Comtesse determined to gain his aim.

The Duc de Rohan-Chabot was now constantly with the Comtesse. He knew only too well how defenceless she stood. Yet he also knew that the more actively he intervened for her safety the worse he made the case. Many friends disappeared, often never to be heard of again. Those of certain importance had a trial or mock trial, but the less known were got rid of quickly and unobtrusively. There was no time or wish to bother about them. Jeanne had ceased walking in the grounds of her property, the villagers had made it unbearable. They were ever crowding around the château shouting abuse. In despair she wrote to the authorities of the county, imploring their aid. She was frightened by the incessant demonstrations around herself. She asked in the name of humanity to have all this stopped, but it was too late, Greive and Blache had won the day.

The Committee decreed that the woman named Du Barry living at Louveciennes be arrested as a traitor for her dealings with the aristocracy, and taken to the prison of Sainte-Pélagie in Paris and be kept there as a measure of general safety. Seals would be placed on her belongings and a search would be made in her papers. Those of subversive contents would be brought to the Comité de Sûreté Générale. To assist in the arrest Greive was authorized to engage any power, to the extent of the Army. The arrest would include all those residing under the roof of Louveciennes, the document was signed by Boucher-Saint-Sauveur, Amar, Vadier, and Panis.

21

Arrest

It was seven o'clock in the morning of the 21st of September 1793 when Jeanne Du Barry opened her window. It promised to be a lovely day, a slight mist was clinging to the trees, as if loath to leave the beauty of Louveciennes. Jeanne seemed to be searching the horizon. Was she endeavouring to discover a way of escape if the *sans-culottes* became too dangerous? But she felt safe for the present, was her enchanting Rohan-Chabot not watching over her? An hour later she was dressed and writing letters. The Duc had had to leave for Paris the evening before but would return that night. She was musing, her pen lay idle between her fingers, she wondered if her beloved Brissac would have been sad at the idea that someone had taken his place. Yet she felt sure that his love for her was so above worldly things, and he would be happy that she was not alone. After all, this episode was so different from his, he had been a lover of the spirit as well as of the flesh. This liaison was of the flesh and little of the spirit. As she went on musing, far away from the fear of the moment, the sound of heavy feet came up the delicate staircase, and bursting into her room without knocking, Greive stood there at the head of a company of soldiers, her heart stopped.

'What do you want?' she called out.

'We have come to arrest you and all those we find in this house, no one can escape, all doors are guarded.'

Suddenly the awful thought came to her, all her private papers, which she had intended to destroy were lying on a table in her bedroom. She rushed to open a secret door which led to a small staircase and from there to her bedroom, that bedroom which had witnessed so many tender scenes. Now a raging ruffian flew into it, she had just grasped the papers and was trying to tear off the signatures. There was a short tussle, but Greive easily pushed her aside and seized the letters and in a rude voice he ordered her to follow him downstairs. The poor woman completely unnerved kept calling for her servants, but they were already in the coach on their way to prison. In a brutal tone and with a mocking laugh Greive told her it was useless to hope to be saved, and without allowing her to take the barest necessities of life, half-pushing, half-dragging, bundled her into the coach. She was unconscious of her surroundings, but one thing seemed to nag her, with a jolt she discovered what it was, 'Who was going to look after her little dog Tintin?'

Near Bougival, Monsieur d'Escourre was passing in a small cabriolet. Grieve ordered him to stop, arrested him, and forced him to get into the coach. Such had become the power of those in authority that its every member could act on his own initiative and satisfy the ravings of his hatred.

Up to now very little news had been allowed to filter through concerning Marie Antoinette. Jeanne Du Barry had often volunteered to offer sums of money to aid the Queen in her distress, but she had been advised to wait, any indiscretion might worsen Her Majesty's position. As Monsieur d'Escourre took a seat next to Jeanne, he told her that he knew now for certain that Marie Antoinette had been transferred from the Temple to the Conciergerie, and was living in a damp basement cell, whose walls were steaming with moisture, and had its tiny window totally obscured by years of dirt. Her son had been taken away from her and even forced to testify against his mother. Many plans had been attempted by courageous friends to save her but none had succeeded. Her pride had kept her alive and for her children's sake she had wished to live. As Monsieur d'Escourre told all this to Jeanne, it gave her untold courage; she also would fight for her life!

Once again, and for the third time Jeanne was entering a prison gate. Sainte-Pélagie was one of the most gruesome prisons of France. From there hundreds had been forced to make their last journey and to bend their heads under the knife of the guillotine for the so-called justice of the Revolution. Somehow the prison had an odour of despair and an ugliness of doom. Madame Roland, in her memoirs describes the inside of the building. 'Sainte-Pélagie is divided into long stone corridors, on either side of which are small bare mildewed cells, each one is closed by a huge padlock which is securely fastened at night. In one corner of the cell lies a sodden straw mattress covered by a stained blanket, in the other corner stands a stool and a revolting pail for private use. There is a rusty nail left on the wall on which a crucifix must have hung, but this holy emblem has long since been taken down.' When Jeanne was led into this hole she thanked the gendarme for his kindness, in a dazed state she had completely lost sense of things. She sat on the grimy stool and waited, there was nothing else she could do. Later an old woman brought her a piece of bread and a jug of water, she ate and drank reluctantly. For a long time she hesitated, looking at the nauseating scarcely covered straw, but eventually, utterly worn out, she lay on it without undressing and slept. She had not even a *fichu* to put around her head.

At dawn came a rattle on the door, a soldier unlocked it, and barked, 'Arouse yourself.' When Jeanne stepped out of that slimy ill-smelling cell she was confronted by a crowd of women in all conditions filling the huge spaces, the corridors, the staircases, the courtyard, and all talking and waiting. To her amazement there were several ladies she recognized, duchesses and marquises among them, Mesdames de Gouy, de Montmorency, de Moncrif, as well as the nine most celebrated actresses of the Théâtre Français. Jeanne tried to reach the ladies she knew; they had taken refuge in the yard but she could not move, being hemmed in by the crowd of smelly unwashed women. Many prostitutes surrounded her, she had no difficulty in determining their trade, they must have been some of the lowest in Paris, she assumed, as they talked amongst themselves in the brutal tone of the streets. One wonders if the revolting chatter of those whores made her conscious of her past, but all that was so remote that as they brushed by her she drew herself away. Soon a booming gong sounded – it was time to regain the cells. Jostling and pushing they went back to their 'home', until the following morning when the whole performance would be repeated. She was never able to speak to those whom she knew. In her solitude she wrote a letter to Henriette Couture, one of her maids, who by an oversight had not been arrested, and had been left at Louveciennes. It revealed Jeanne's courage and fortitude, as she could not write to Rohan-Chabot she hoped he would get news of her through this woman.

'I am well, I found here what I needed, give me news of those who are with you. Have they put seals everywhere? Have the inhabitants formulated a petition for my return? Please send me a bonnet of muslin, also some chemises, white or blue, some handkerchiefs, and all you can send me. I need some *fichus* also, and a dozen towels and sheets. Tell the villagers that I am well. Mlle. Roussel and her companions are at La Force prison. I have no one to defend me as yet. Please take care of Tintin.'

Jeanne Du Barry felt assured in her innermost self she would be released after a few days, she was certain that her Rohan-Chabot was working for her freedom. She longed for a word from him, but knew that for her sake he must abstain from any apparent knowledge of her whereabouts.

As Jeanne stood in that stifling atmosphere of women she observed that each morning some of those whom she had noticed the morning before were missing. She questioned one of the guards standing by:

'Have some of the ladies who were in the yard yesterday been released?'

With a sneer the guard answered, 'Those no-goods were taken away in the night. Today they have a busy day at the guillotine and work had to begin before dawn.'

The days were passing, the monotony was suffocating, alone! alone! For a short time a young woman had been lodged in her cell, she had been told there was no other room, the prison was overflowing. The girl was a simple person, but Jeanne was pleased to have someone to speak to. Her companion did not know the reason for her incarceration. One morning she was fetched; Jeanne never saw her again. Notwithstanding all she heard and saw, she had great hopes for her own freedom, she was so sure of success that failure did not enter her mind. But times had changed, all chivalry, all pity, all understanding had been crushed and only cruelty and a desire for blood seemed to emanate from all sides, 'Sadism' was the password. Jeanne would have felt less secure if she had known that her banker Vandenyver, father and sons, had been arrested and that their records, papers and lists of customers' names had been seized. All their secret transactions with the Comtesse Du Barry would come to light, the huge funds which had been constantly transferred to England for her account and which would reveal that they had been devoted to the Royalist cause.

On the 22nd of September, the day after her arrest, Greive and Blache, aided by Zamor and the valet Sanalave, whom Jeanne had dismissed, went to Louveciennes. They broke all the seals, and brutally ransacked drawers, boxes and chests. They discovered many secret hiding-places in which money, jewellery and valuables of every kind had been hidden. A quantity of silver was found in a shed where the gardener kept his tools, the famous gold dinner-service, diamonds and emeralds were found under the straw in the stables. In Mlle. Roussel's powder-box was hidden the medal which William Pitt had presented to Madame Du Barry. A great number of the pieces which had been listed as part of the robbery were unearthed from under the floor boards. Then in a special receptacle bundles and bundles of letters, papers and pamphlets were uncovered. All these were read and annotated for her trial, Greive was accumulating every detail of her past life, document after document was being prepared by him and Blache – some true, some untrue. Her association with the *émigrés*, her liaison with the *ci-devant* Duc de Brissac, her journeys to England, the excuse of the famous robbery which could now be proven never to have taken place. It had been just a subterfuge to reside in England in order to aid the enemies of the people. Unbeknown to Jeanne Du Barry the hour of her trial was nearing.

22

The Trial

It was now almost a month since Madame Du Barry entered Sainte-Pélagie, her optimism was becoming fainter. The inmates were disappearing more rapidly, it seemed to take only one or two days for them to be driven to their doom. She wrote again to the Convention pleading for her release, but no answer came. She had been sent a few clothes by Henriette, which she was able to wash with the small amount of water allowed. One supposes that the sudden change from the unbelievable luxury in which she had been encased to the basest level of subsistence had numbed her sensibilities, otherwise she would have succumbed. But all this was revived in all its horror and bitterness, when on the 16th of October 1793 the guard, bringing the soup and bread said in a casual voice, 'Marie Antoinette was executed this morning, one less enemy for France.'

On the 30th of October, two members of the Comité de Sûreté Générale arrived at Sainte-Pélagie charged with the interrogation of the citoyenne Du Barry. Jeanne was taken to a room where stood the *citoyens* Voulland and Jagot, they looked unkempt and had an indefinable smell about them. There were several chairs around the room, but neither of them asked her to sit down, so all stood. They delved right down in her relations with Louis XV, her expenditure, into the help she had given to the *émigrés*. They urged her to admit that the jewel robbery had only been a ruse planned with Forth, the British agent, with a view to aiding the counter revolutionaries in England. Jeanne denied this, and answered calmly and without reservation. The names of her friends were put to her as counter revolutionaries, the Chevalier d'Escourre, the Duc de Rohan-Chabot, Monsieur de Calonne, the Princesse Lubomirska, and the Duc de Brissac. Her continued calmness impressed her inquisitors. Many of the events mentioned she could not deny, the proofs were too obvious. Two days later the same agents, Voulland and Jagot repaired to the La Force prison, where the bankers Vandenyver were detained. They were interrogated, every question concerning Madame Du Barry's connection with them was reviewed. Monsieur Vandenyver was discreet but the papers were there to testify to the huge transactions.

The Comité de Sûreté Générale decided to accelerate the trials which were still lagging behind. Looking over the long lists they discovered in their holocaust of victims the *citoyenne* Du Barry and her banker accomplice Vandenyver. So hurriedly they resolved to order that the accused should be interrogated immediately by the Tribunal Revolutionnaire. The questioning took place on the 22nd of November in the presence of the Vice-President Dumas, and the Public Prosecutor Fouquier-Tinville. On the morning of that day Jeanne wondered why the prison guard had not unlocked her door for the customary outing, but soon her wonder was changed to alarm when a dozen armed men entered her cell and the officer in charge ordered her to follow them to the Palais de Justice. It was cold, she wrapped her coat around her shoulders and, too alarmed to protest, followed them through the long corridors down the stone staircase. As her feeling of panic increased she commenced to tremble, she could not control herself. The shock of the sudden intrusion of these men, the idea of the Palais de Justice, the sight of the outer world after the long imprisonment, unnerved her. The officer evidently took pity on her and drawing himself close to her said, 'Do not fear, Madame.' Then moving away quickly he shouted in a loud voice so as to be heard by his men, 'Faster, we are in a hurry.' When she and her escort reached the enormous building of the Palais de Justice she felt calm. Those words 'Do not fear, Madame' had restored her hope of deliverance. She was taken up a monumental staircase along an endless corridor. At length they reached the doors of the Court, which were thrown open with a crash. As the small group of soldiers leading Jeanne Du Barry entered she was taken to one of the benches reserved for the prisoners. The great hall seemed empty, except on her left where the *commissaires* were sitting at a long table. Among those presiding she noticed two men, the Vice-President Dumas, and the sinister looking Fouquier-Tinville, the Public Prosecutor. The former had no distinguishing feature, he seemed only to preside and looked not particularly interested, but the latter, even before uttering a syllable exuded terror. He was a dark-haired man, with heavy shaggy eyebrows, small round shrewd eyes, low forehead, full face with a deadly white complexion. He was powerfully built, had a good figure, and seemed sure of his power. Jeanne was told to approach, this interrogation was only of a preliminary nature, the real trial would come later. As Fouquier-Tinville questioned her on the same subjects as Jagot and Voulland had done, Jeanne gave the same answers, dignified, truthful and courageous. In the midst of this cross-examination the doors opened and the banker Vandenyver, followed by his two sons, appeared surrounded by an armed escort: he and Madame Du Barry exchanged glances. Immediately they were questioned, mostly concerning the large sums of money they had supplied to *la femme* Du Barry. They replied with the utmost caution, for the questions were fraught with pitfalls. Nevertheless they could not deny the accusations, 'they' held the proofs. At last the interrogation seemed to be nearing its end, Dumas had already risen from his seat, Fouquier-Tinville was gathering his papers. Jeanne and the Vandenyvers felt relieved – it might have been worse. She picked up her coat which had fallen on the ground, when Fouquier-Tinville spoke – 'I wish the accused to be transferred to the Conciergerie.' There was complete silence; even Dumas looked startled, but he bowed his head in acquiescence.

La Conciergerie! The very name made people shrink within themselves as something unholy, as the brand of 'the end of hope.' The escort closed around Jeanne, and she was once more taken along that corridor, once or twice she stumbled but no one offered to hold her up. Then the thought came to her, 'Why should I fear, the Queen went through all this and more, she had children, I have only myself.' Marie Antoinette had been given strength and courage by her great faith, but Jeanne was not so fervent, she had no strong belief to turn to, she felt alone. She had brought nothing with her from Sainte-Pélagie, but the officer of the escort again approached her as she stepped into the carriage and said, 'You will be helped.' As the coach passed through the huge massive doors of the Conciergerie Jeanne Du Barry entered her last prison. A grim wardress with a stern hard look stood waiting, she dismissed the escort saying, 'There is no danger of escape, you can leave.' The officer tried to approach Jeanne, who was gruffly told to go down below. It seemed to Jeanne that the descent would never end, it grew darker and darker, and the smell of damp mouldy walls nearly choked her, still they went down. At last two men came along with torches and showed the way to her cell. The wardress said as she opened the heavy iron door, 'As a Royalist you will be interested to know that this is where your Queen Marie Antoinette lived, and from here she went to her death.' The woman did not say this unkindly, the Queen's charm and fortitude had touched all hearts. 'You will be allowed a candle, and your food will be given to you.' As she was leaving she re-opened the door and added, 'Your clothes will be brought to you tomorrow, it is too late tonight.' For the first time in her life Jeanne fell on her knees of her own free will and prayed first for the Queen, whom she would have loved to have served, and then for herself to be given the same strength that had been accorded to Marie Antoinette. The stump of the tallow candle was flickering, but as her eyes became accustomed to the darkness, she could not restrain a cry of horror at the sight of the narrow hole in which she found herself. The smell of the rotting straw which covered the stone floor, mixed with the mildew from the moss-covered walls and the lack of oxygen almost suffocated her. She looked in vain for a window, but what resembled such a thing was too high to reach and so covered by dirt that it could never have been opened. Jeanne Du Barry rose at dawn the next day, the smell seemed stronger, it had pervaded her whole system. The same wardress of the evening before brought her some hot soup and a loaf of bread. It was welcome, Jeanne required something to sustain her. A little later the woman brought her the clothes from Sainte-Pélagie, Jeanne chose only a few pieces – there was no room to put the rest. In a callous tone the wardress said, 'Your final trial is for today at nine o'clock.' Jeanne asked what the time was. 'It is now half past five.'

That morning at the break of day one of the most courageous acts in history took place. The wardress's last words seemed to freeze Jeanne's whole being. So at last the dreaded moment had arrived; in a few hours she would learn her fate, but she already knew what it would be. Her answers would produce such terrible results for so many people, denial would be in vain, the prosecution held the names already. Perhaps the one she feared the most for was the Duchesse de Mortemart, daughter of the Duc de Brissac, who had wished that they should become sisters. What could she do to rescue her? There came a discreet knock at the iron door, slowly it was opened and a man walked in, she rose frightened, gently he pushed the door behind him and coming up to her said, 'Fear not, Madame La Comtesse, I am a priest, I am Irish, and have not sworn allegiance to the Convention. So far I have not been arrested and can help the afflicted, I have not much time before me, so we must not lose a moment. I have come with a plan for your escape, I have heard that your trial is for today, this is your only chance to live, there is no other hope. I can carry this out if you can provide me with a sum of money so as to bribe the guards.' For a few seconds Jeanne was silent, then she asked him:

'Can you save two people?'

'No,' he answered. 'My plan only allows for one person.'

'In that case,' answered Madame Du Barry, 'I shall give an order on my banker for the necessary sum of money. I am prepared to go to my death, but I ask you to save a person very dear to me.'

The priest still urged her to save herself, he would manage to get her away. Once more she repeated her question, 'Can you save two people?' With tears in his eyes he shook his head then he looked at his watch – 'We must hurry.' Then Jeanne made her supreme decision.

'In that case you must save the Duchesse de Mortemart; she is hiding in an attic in Calais, this is the name she is using and her address.'

The priest pleaded, 'But Madame la Comtesse do you realize what lies before you? Save yourself!'

Jeanne did not answer but hastily wrote an order on her bank, and said, 'When you see her, tell her that I offer my life in remembrance of her father.'

The dreaded hour of nine was approaching, the priest with his eyes full of tears asked her to kneel and blessing her said, 'No greater love can a man show than to lay down his life for a friend,' and opening the heavy door, faded away in the dark.

Once again her escort stood waiting to lead her to that 'Hall' of so-called justice. As she entered the Court she stood irresolute, how could she face that multitude of faces? Then she remembered the Queen, it gave her the strength to proceed. Every seat of that notorious Hall was occupied, people were standing close to one another. It was not an everyday event which was to occur, but the trial of the famous and infamous mistress of Louis XV, the woman who by her licentious life had almost ruined France. She reached her bench where Vandenyver and his two sons were already seated, she glanced at the judges. Dumas and Fouquier-Tinville were present, almost hemmed in by the witnesses. She observed Zamor, that child whom she had cherished, and Sanalave who had been in her service for twenty years. Henriette Couture, and Mlle. Roussel were well to the fore as were Greive and Blache, they were all there and many more. For a time one could only hear the murmur of countless whispered conversations, even the judges spoke in very low tones. Vandenyver and his sons were a little way away from her so she could not speak to them. The defence had been assigned to the advocates Chauveau-Lagarde and Lafleuterie, Dumas, the Vice-President, was acting as President. Fouquier-Tinville had made sure that the jury was composed of staunch Republicans, all seemed in order and yet the seance had not begun. The time seemed long, the accused were still sitting waiting to know their fate. The noise became almost deafening; all the spectators were discussing the case among themselves, and giving their opinion as to the probable decision of the judges. Suddenly three loud raps resounded like a deathknell, and a powerful voice called out:

'Silence in Court!'

Everyone in the immense Hall seemed to have become dumb, not even a cough could be heard. Once more the powerful voice called out:

'The accused are to approach.'

Jeanne, the beautiful Comtesse Du Barry, was now facing the men who had the power to grant her life or death. Many of those who were now staring at this figure of the past could scarcely recognize her, and yet notwithstanding all that she was going through, she still possessed a ray of that beauty which had astonished the world. The powerful voice rose again in question.

'What is your name?'

'Jeanne Vaubernier Du Barry.'

'Where were you born?'

'At Vaucouleurs in Lorraine.'

'What is your age?'

'I am forty-two.'

Even at this fatal moment her coquetry made her declare herself as five years younger than she was.

'Where do you live?'

'At Louveciennes.'

Then turning to the Vandenyvers,

'What is your name?'

'Jean Baptiste Vandenyver, Dutch banker.'

'Where were you born?'

'In Paris.'

'What is your age?'

'I am sixty-six.'

Then the same questions were put to each of his sons, Edmé-Jean-Baptiste Vandenyver, thirty-two and Antoine-Augustin Vandenyver, twenty-nine years old.

Fouquier-Tinville was standing on the second step of the

tribune, he was leaning on two large boxes which contained the evidence. The four accused stood rigid, not a tremor could be noticed.

'Femme Du Barry, come closer.'

Jeanne took a few steps forward, the other three a few steps backwards. At this moment Greive was told to give his evidence.

'I wish to testify that the Du Barry tried to prevent the enlistment of troops at Louveciennes. In her property were found buried in different places quantities of valuable articles. Many of these had been stated as stolen when the great jewel robbery took place at Louveciennes. The celebrated gold dinner-service, gems, emeralds, gold coins, were found where the gardeners kept their tools, and among bronze ornaments the bust of Louis XV. In her maid's room, hidden in a powder-box was a medal which William Pitt had presented to her. The Du Barry had several residences in Paris, where she openly and also secretly met *émigrés* and their relations. The spy Forth was constantly coming and going from her abodes to England. Her mysterious visits to that country were suspicious. She gave the excuse of the robbery, when first interrogated, and admitted that the trial for her jewels was over in March 1793. Why then did she still require a passport to return to England on account of the trial which she stated was still pending?'

At this point Jeanne protested,

'My journey was necessary to receive the diamonds and pay the advocate's fees.'

Xavier Audoin, another witness was called to certify that during one of his house searches at Louveciennes a *ci-devant* named Maussabré was discovered in a room of the accused.

Now Blache was called to give evidence, fluently the fruits of all his spying came forth. Her every action in London was recorded, the people she entertained, those whom she had helped secretly, the detailed account of the valuables found hidden at Louveciennes; all done to defraud the loyal Republican people from their due and to benefit the enemies of liberty. Her intimate friendship with the British spy, Forth. Several letters had been found from him, some words had been erased, every minor detail was mentioned, exaggerated, amplified. The people in the Hall were breathlessly silent, Fouquier-Tinville continued taking notes. Still Jeanne was standing alone, with the other three accused just behind her. Monsieur d'Escourre was brought in, he stood to one side while being questioned. He was asked concerning the sums of money which had passed through his hands to Madame Du Barry. Unfortunately he became mixed up in his replies and trying to vindicate Jeanne implicated her irretrievably, ending by destroying the little hope there was left. Fouquier-Tinville ordered his transfer from La Force to the Conciergerie, which meant his end. Jeanne felt exhausted, but stood outwardly calm. Fouquier-Tinville deciding to probe her to the very depth of her being, asked her if she could deny having been the mistress of Louis XV the tyrant, and Brissac the traitor, and other enemies of the glorious Republic. She seemed to gather new strength.

'No,' she answered, 'I was Louis XV's mistress, and I am proud to have been, and also of Brissac. The others only concern myself.'

Then Zamor and Sanalave stood near her, she closed her eyes, she could not look at them, especially Zamor. They testified brutally against her, she had received and written letters to the men fighting against France, and had paid large sums to maintain their armies. She tried to protest.

'All this is untrue,' she cried, 'Zamor my little one, how can you lie against me, you whom I have loved as my own child.'

But no one listened; the noise had started again, the people were crying for vengeance. Dumas banged his hammer and shouted to them to cease their noise but they were out of hand and did not even hear him. At last they were tired and stopped. Mlle. Roussel and Henriette Couture were called; they were shaking with fright, their testimony was that the Comtesse had torn up some letters after the Duc de Brissac's arrest. For having mentioned the title 'Comtesse' and 'Duc' they were threatened with imprisonment.

Jeanne was told to step back and the three Vandenyvers were instructed to come forward. The questioning restarted, but with the object of proving that they had advanced money to the Du

Barry knowing the purpose for which it would be employed, viz. to re-establish once again the tyrannical reign of the Monarchy. All their protestations of innocence were waved aside, it was useless, all the proofs were in the files of the Convention. At that moment Fouquier-Tinville rose from his seat, in his left hand he held a bundle of notes, he advanced slightly and summoned the accused to stand in line before him. Jeanne was almost sinking but she stood bravely, she forced herself to remember the Queen, who had gone through all this. The Queen had had no hope but perhaps she might have a chance. Then the prosecutor began his final indictment. The advocate Chauveau-Lagarde who was supposed to defend the accused, tried to make an effort to say a few words in the defence of his clients, but he was pushed aside and Fouquier-Tinville proceeded to address the jury:

'Members of the Jury, you have already given your verdict on the spouse of the last of the tyrants of France. Now you are asked to pronounce your verdict one way or another on the courtesan of his infamous predecessor. You see standing before you this Laïs celebrated for her dissolute morals and the publicity and brilliance given to her debauchery. Her lewdness alone has enabled her to acquire a large share of the wealth of France, which has been built and gathered by the sacrifice and the blood of the people, all to satisfy her shameful pleasures. The scandal of her elevation and the turpitude of her infamous prostitution are not the principal reason for your verdict. You are to decide if this Messalina born of the people, enriched by the spoils of the people, who by their poverty paid for her high rank, is guilty of conspiracy against their liberty. Later, after the death of the "Tyrant", she led her own life, plotting against the freedom and sovereignty of the people. She became the agent of conspirators, of nobles, of priests. We are in no doubt as to the truth of all these facts. It is clear that now stands before you the source from which William Pitt and all his accomplices conceived their plans and plots against France. It was useful to have put before you the details of the conspiracies in which the courtesan and her associates took part.

Such are, members of the jury, the incriminating results of the cross-examinations which have taken place. It is now for you to weigh them in your great wisdom. You can judge for yourselves that the Royalists, the Federalists and all these factions, apparently divided, had the same ends. The war, the Vendée troubles, the unrest in the south, the insurrection in Calvados, all sprang from the same principle and were commanded by two leaders, d'Artois and Pethion, all working under the order of William Pitt. Yes, Frenchmen, we swear the traitors will perish, France will triumph over the power of the priests and infamous courtesans. The degraded woman who stands before you, whose opulence allowed her to act against the liberty of the people must be struck down in the name of the law. In doing so you will not only avenge the Republic but will condemn publicly the scandal which she caused, and affirm the law of decent morals, which is the first base of the Empire of the people.'

This speech of the Public Prosecutor, full of hate, had little effect on the jury, they had already reached their decision. Once again the advocates tried to speak in defence of the accused, but it was too late, no further pleading could sway the jury's determination. In a few words the President delivered his summing-up, the jury rose and retired to agree or disagree on the verdict. The prisoners were led out of the Court, taken to a room, and told to wait – they would be called again shortly.

The crowd relaxed and started eating the food they had brought. The judges and all the clerks left the Court, all would return later for the final scene.

In that small room the four accused were offered a glass of water. The three men, the father and his two sons were silent. After a while the younger one whispered:

'But Fouquier-Tinville did not mention our names in his indictment, perhaps we have a chance!'

Then looking at the desolate figure of Jeanne Du Barry he said, 'I fear for her.' Pale-faced, Jeanne sat with her eyes closed, her hands pressed together, Vandenyver drew near her and kneeling on one knee took her hand and raised it to his lips, 'Courage Madame, it may be easier than we think!' Slowly the door of that tiny room was opened and one of the clerks called out in an un-emotional voice:

'The accused are requested to re-enter the Court.' Vandenyver seeing Madame Du Barry almost unable to leave her seat, came to her rescue and supporting her, he walked towards the Court, the two young men followed. The Hall seemed fuller than ever. Once more the woman and the three men stood facing their fate. President Dumas, Fouquier-Tinville, Chauveau-Lagarde the advocate who had tried to speak on their behalf, were there. All the witnesses were present, Zamor, Sanalave, Blache and Greive. Vandenyver was thrust away from Jeanne, she looked around, faces, faces, faces, grimacing with hate – no one who would inter-cede for mercy. But the Queen had stood erect, she must stand erect too. At this moment the jury filed in, she heard the voice of Dumas but could not catch his words, only one reached her ears, 'Guilty.' The jury had made their decision! Fouquier-Tinville came forward and in a voice which echoed in the furthermost part of the Hall declared:

'Jeanne Vaubernier Du Barry, living at Louveciennes, former courtesan is convicted of being one of the accomplices of those enemies of France who conspired for her ruin. The bankers, Jean-Baptiste Vandenyver, domiciled in Paris, Edmé-Jean-Baptiste Vandenyver, and Antoine-Augustin Vandenyver both of Paris are convicted of being accomplices of the enemies of France who conspired for her ruin. The aforementioned Jeanne Vauber-nier, the Du Barry woman, Jean-Baptiste Vandenyver, Edmé-Jean-Baptiste Vandenyver and Antoine-Augustin Vandenyver are condemned

TO DEATH

23

The Last Obeisance

There was a muffled sound, the Comtesse Du Barry had fainted. All at once pandemonium broke out, the crowd clapped their hands with excitement and delight, but a few isolated voices shouted, 'It is plain murder.' Jeanne could hear none of the night-mare, a gendarme carried her back to her cavern in the Conciergerie and left her. The Vandenyvers were escorted to their cells to live through a night of terror and despair. As the guards left Jeanne the prison clock struck eleven, the execution was for next morning at eleven o'clock at the Place de la Révolution. A large contingent of armed forces had been ordered to attend in view of the dis-turbance in Court. Jeanne was blessed by being almost un-conscious all that night. The wardress came to her about five o'clock in the morning, and told her to sit up, she was going to cut off her hair in preparation for the forthcoming event. Jeanne seemed to revive. 'Oh! not my hair!' The wardress with a pitying glance said, 'But my poor lady how could the executioner work if your neck was not bare?' So those beautiful locks gradually fell on the stone floor. A freezing chill went through Jeanne and large tears rolled down her cheeks. Then feeling that this woman who had done the same job many, many times and yet had a heart, might help her, she asked, 'Did you assist the Queen on that night which was her last?'

'Yes,' answered the woman.

'Tell me something about her, to give me courage.'

'All I can tell you is that she was the bravest of them all, her faith in God was very great and it gave her the strength to go to her death. Yes, she is an example to all those who have to face their end on the scaffold.'

Jeanne asked the time and the date, the woman looked at her

massive silver watch and said, 'It is half past five, and today is the 8th of December,' and picking up those beautiful tresses, which lay on the floor like souvenirs of the past, she left.

At seven o'clock the wardress re-entered the cell to wake the prisoner, but seeing that her eyes were closed, she decided to come back later. At eight o'clock she returned, Jeanne was still in the same position. She shook her, Jeanne Du Barry raised herself; seeing the wardress the agony of reality flooded her mind, and in an instant she looked ten years older. Then a sudden idea dawned on her, she would reveal the hiding-place of the treasures that had not yet been found, and where her jewels, which were left in England, could be located. She would divulge the names of the people who had helped her. At that moment the iron door slid back and Samson, the executioner accompanied by an officer and several armed soldiers, entered. Samson was carrying a long rope, without any word being spoken he pulled Jeanne up from her chair, and roughly tied her hands behind her back. He held on to the end of the rope so that she could not get away. From then on she lost all control, struggling, weeping, shouting, 'If they grant me my life, I will disclose where all my treasures are hidden, and will give up my remaining fortune to the State. I will also name the people who hold my jewels.' She had become frantic, Samson was startled, he was unaccustomed to such scenes. As they arrived at one of the wicket-gates of the Conciergerie, Madame Du Barry continued to shout and repeat the same phrases over and over again. At this gate an official was stationed to record her departure for the Place de la Révolution. In her fever she clung to him describing in halting phrases all the details of the objects hidden, where they could be found, and who had the custody of her jewels in England. She was ready to sign away her fortune, only let her live. The official, taken unawares, decided to send for a superior, and Jeanne was ushered into a small waiting-room. So as to encourage her confidences, the officer who had taken over from the baffled official, made her understand that it might influence her release if she made a full confession. The poor woman did not realize that she had given away all her secrets without saving her life. All this had taken time and it was now half past four in the afternoon and already getting dark in the badly lit streets of old Paris. Jeanne still retained a faint hope that all her revelations might have saved her. Yet desperation enveloped her completely when the doors of the Conciergerie drew back and there stood the ominous tumbril. She was lifted into it by her executioner, he flung her on to a wooden board which served as a seat. Vandenyver and his two sons climbed in behind her. Jeanne Du Barry sank into a heap, she was deathly white, Samson was still holding the rope. The small escort closed round and the horses slowly started to walk. It was a Sunday, in the streets the people were waiting eagerly, they had done so for hours, although the weather was cold and raw, and slight flecks of snow were falling. Vandenyver glanced at the once dazzling Comtesse Du Barry, now a miserable specimen of humanity in prison clothes, going to her death. The crowd jeered, intent only on her; the others meant nothing to them. Jeanne seemed unaware of her surroundings. As the jolting cart went over the cobbled streets nearing the Place de la Révolution the mob increased. Up to this Jeanne had sat with closed eyes, now she opened them, and the realization that there was no escape and nothing and nobody could rescue her made her lose all sense. She rose from that board and tried to throw herself out of the tumbril. Vandenyver grabbed her, but she was beyond hearing his voice, she screamed, she tried to wrench herself away. The two young Vandenyvers held on to her, Samson who still held the end of the rope came to their aid. By now all dignity had left her, her cries, her screams, her hiccuping phrases for mercy could be heard all down the Rue St. Honoré and beyond. The people were startled, some were applauding, some were praying. They had never seen such a display of fear. All the others they had witnessed, had gone to their death calmly almost smiling. 'But then,' said an old woman to another, 'they all had an ideal, a faith, the pride of their name, which is linked with history. This poor whore has nothing, but her wretched life.' Years ago, when the Empress Marie-Therese, urged her daughter Marie Antoinette to tolerate her grandfather's mistress, the same meaning had been expressed in different words. 'Remember this poor woman, although possessing all, in reality has nothing.'

At last the distracted creature's journey was ending. The tumbril had reached the steps of the imposing, terrifying guillotine. The massive steel blade waiting to be released could be discerned by the flickering light of the torches around. Jeanne shook wildly at the monstrous sight. Vandenyver and his two sons remained calm, still trying to comfort her, but she had lost all semblance of reason. Samson carelessly threw to his *aide* the rope he was still holding, and bade him carry her to the block while he adjusted the machine. The man lifted her and started on his ghastly pilgrimage – the rope still trailing behind them. Jeanne suddenly lay quite still, she had fought to live but she had lost the struggle. As the knife was ready to do its gruesome work in a last spasm Jeanne gave a cry which resembled no human sound.

✣   ✣   ✣

The sacrifice was accomplished. The crash of the knife which ended the Comtesse Du Barry's life also destroyed one of the last remnants of that era of Versailles, with all the splendour, grace, refinement of the eighteenth century which will never be revived. She had known the direst poverty and the height of power. She had engendered insane hatred, and been adored to the point of idolatry. In reality she was an enigma, but who can judge another's life! 'Let him without sin cast the first stone.'

Bibliography

Moufle d'Angerville: *La vie privée de Louis XV*.

Marquis d'Argenson: *Mémoires*.

Joseph Aulneau: *La Comtesse Du Barry et la fin de l'ancien régime*.

Barbey d'Aurevilly: *Les oeuvres et les hommes*.

La Bastide (de): *La présentation à la cour de la Comtesse Du Barry*.

Louis-J. de Bouillé: *Souvenirs et fragments*.

Cabanés (docteur): *L'Enfer de l'Histoire*.

Madame Campan: *La vie privée de Marie Antoinette*.

Fr. Castanié: *Les royales amours d'une petite modiste*.

Capefigue: *Mme. Du Barry (les reines de la main gauche)*.

J. de Cayeux: *Le pavillon de Mme. Du Barry à Louveciennes et son architecte Ledoux*.

Comte de Cheverny: *Souvenirs et mémoires*.

Duc de Choiseul: *Mémoires*.

J. T. d'Espinchal: *Procés de Mme. Du Barry*.

Flammermont: *Correspondance des agents diplomatiques étrangers*.

Comte Fleury: *Fantômes et silhouettes*.

P. Fromageot: *Mme. Du Barry de 1791 à 1793*.

Gastone: *Les nuits galantes de Louis XV*.

Ed. and J. de Goncourt: *La Du Barry*.

Pierre Gaxotte: *Le siécle de Louis XV*.

Arséne Houssaye: *L'Histoire de Mme. Du Barry*.

Duc de Lauzun: *Mémoires*.

G. Lenôtre: *Paris revolutionnaire*.

A. Leroy: *Madame Du Barry et son temps*.

Prince Charles de Ligne: *Mémoires*.

Louis Madelin: *La France de Louis XV*.

Gaston Maugras: *Le duc et la duchesse de Choiseul*.

Pierre de Nolhac: *Marie Antoinette et Madame Du Barry. Le château de Versailles sous Louis XV. Louis XV et Marie Leczinska. Les appartements de Mme. Du Barry.*

Reiset: *Grandes dames.*

Duc de Richelieu: *Mémoires du maréchal de Richelieu.*

Imbert de St-Amand: *La cour de Louis XV.*

Claude St-André: *Madame Du Barry.*

H. Stein: *Pajou et Mme. Du Barry.*

Prince de Talleyrand: *Mémoires.*

C. Vatel: *Histoire de Mme. Du Barry. Mme Du Barry et son temps.*

Madame Vigée-Lebrun: *Mémoires.*

Walpole-du-Deffand: *Correspondence.*

H. Welchinger: *Les bijoux de Mme. Du Barry.*

Index

Index

Index